Lifesaver Lessons™
LANGUAGE ARTS
GRADE 4

T5-DHC-027

What Are Lifesaver Lessons?

Lifesaver Lessons™ are everything you need to deliver a well-planned lesson at a moment's notice. Lifesaver Lessons are curriculum-based lesson plans that include:

- Easy steps and materials needed
- Ideas for introducing the lessons
- Reproducible activities and patterns
- Extension ideas

Project Editor:
Peggy Hambright

Editor:
Irving P. Crump

Writers:
Julie Alarie, Colleen Dabney,
Peggy W. Hambright, Terry Healy,
Debra Liverman, Cathy Ogg,
Stephanie Willett-Smith

Artists:
Jennifer Tipton Bennett,
Cathy Spangler Bruce, Clevell Harris,
Rob Mayworth, Barry Slate, Donna K. Teal

Cover Artist:
Jennifer Tipton Bennett

Table Of Contents

Grammar

Writing

Reading

Answer Keys 95

©1997 by THE EDUCATION CENTER, INC.
All rights reserved except as here noted.

Except as provided for herein, no part of this publication may be reproduced or transmitted in any form or by any means, electronic or mechanical, including photocopying, recording, or storing in any information storage and retrieval system or electronic on-line bulletin board, without prior written permission from The Education Center, Inc. Permission is given to the original purchaser to reproduce patterns and reproducibles for individual classroom use only and not for resale or distribution. Reproduction for an entire school or school system is prohibited. Please direct written inquiries to The Education Center, Inc., P.O. Box 9753, Greensboro, NC 27429-0753. The Education Center®, *The Mailbox®*, Lifesaver Lessons™, and the mailbox/post/grass logo are trademarks of The Education Center, Inc., and may be the subject of one or more federal trademark registrations. All other brand or product names are trademarks or registered trademarks of their respective companies. Printed in the United States of America.

Hats Off To Capitalization!

Cap your study of capitalization with this captivating lesson!

Skill: Using capital letters correctly

Estimated Lesson Time: 45 minutes

Teacher Preparation:

1. Duplicate one copy of page 5 for each student.
2. Write the paragraph below on the chalkboard or on a blank transparency with a wipe-off marker.

   the first labor day Parade was held on september 5, 1882, in new york city. since so many people participated in the Events on that day, Officials decided to honor Workers every year. on june 28, 1894, president grover cleveland officially proclaimed the first monday in september as labor day.

Materials:

1 transparency with a paragraph containing capitalization errors
1 wipe-off marker
1 copy of page 5 for each student
crayons
a grammar textbook that lists the rules for capitalization

Background Information:

Capitalization rules govern the use of capital letters. Some words that are always capitalized are:
- proper nouns that name specific persons, places, things, or ideas—the ***D**allas **C**owboys*
- the first word of a sentence—***T**he dog was wet.*
- the pronoun *I*—***I** like hot dogs.*
- the months of the year and the days of the week—***M**ay, **M**onday*
- the first word in both the greeting and the closing of a letter—***D**ear* John, **Y**ours truly
- titles—***P**resident Clinton, **M**rs. Jones, **D**r. Kirk*
- school subjects when they name either a specific language or course—***G**erman, **H**onors **E**nglish*
- geographic locations on a map that refer to specific areas—***M**iddle **E**ast*
- holidays—***S**t. **P**atrick's **D**ay*

Introducing The Lesson:

Begin this lesson by soliciting your students' help. Explain that your friend has asked you to edit an article that he has written for the next issue of your local newspaper. Explain further that you need your students' help with identifying and correcting his capitalization mistakes. Display the transparency that you made; then have a student volunteer read it aloud to the class.

Steps:

1. Call on one student at a time to point out the capitalization errors on the transparency. Require the student to give his reason for capitalizing or not capitalizing a particular word. As a student provides the correct reason, use your wipe-off pen to correct that mistake (see the key on page 95).

2. After your students locate and correct all of the capitalization mistakes on the transparency, have them brainstorm other situations in which capital letters can be used (see page 3 and a grammar textbook that lists capitalization rules). Record your students' responses on the board and discuss them.

3. If desired, challenge your students to cite additional examples for each capitalization rule that you discuss.

4. Give each student a copy of page 5. Direct her to follow the directions on the reproducible for additional practice with capitalization.

• the pronoun *I—I like hot dogs.*

• holidays—*St. Patrick's Day*

Hats Off To Capitalization!

Directions: Read the sentences below one at a time. Decide which words in each sentence should be capitalized and underline them. Then—on the lines underneath each sentence—write brief reasons why capital letters were needed for the words you underlined. If a sentence is correct as it is, color the hat that matches its number!

1. a south american cowboy wears a felt gaucho hat as part of his traditional costume.
   _____
   _____

2. People probably started wearing hats to protect themselves from the weather.
   _____
   _____

3. The Lapps of northern Europe wear snug wool hats that have earflaps.
   _____
   _____

4. A *pelo*—an ancient Greek hat made from wool fibers—is still worn in parts of Siberia today.
   _____
   _____

5. in the 1400s, many women in europe wore a three- to four-foot-tall, veiled, conelike hat known as a *hennin*.
   _____
   _____

6. the height of an amish person's hat—and the width of its brim—revealed whether its wearer was married or not.
   _____
   _____

7. wearing her graduation cap and gown proudly, mrs. jones finally graduated from college at the age of 45.
   _____
   _____

8. people in scotland wear a hat called a *tam-o'-shanter* as part of their traditional dress.
   _____
   _____

9. the first hat factory in the united states was established in 1780 in danbury, connecticut, by zadoc benedict.
   _____
   _____

10. i heard john say that he plans to wear a green hat on st. patrick's day in march.
    _____
    _____

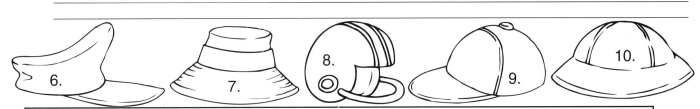

Bonus Box: On the back of this sheet, write the names of as many different hats as you can. Mention five of these hats in sentences that use capital letters correctly.

How To Extend The Lesson:

- Give each student a different newspaper article. Direct the student to circle at least ten words within her article that have been capitalized. Have her assign each capitalized word a number from one to ten. Then have the student number a sheet of paper from one to ten, copy the words onto the paper, and explain why each numbered word requires capitalization.

- Have student volunteers write each capitalization rule on a different sentence strip. Direct another volunteer to make an additional strip that says "No Capitals Needed." Tape the sentence strips to your board, leaving room beneath each strip for placing additional ones. Give each student a blank sentence strip; then instruct him to write a word or phrase on his strip that does or does not need a capital letter. Collect the strips and redistribute them. Then challenge each student in turn to attach his strip to the board underneath its appropriate category with masking tape.

- Distribute envelopes and sheets of stationery to your students. Direct them to copy—spelling all words with lowercase letters—examples of invitations, friendly letters, and fully addressed envelopes from textbooks or reproducibles onto these envelopes and stationery pages. Laminate their examples; then place the stationery in a center along with several wipe-off markers. During free time, challenge your students to find the capitalization errors in each selection and circle them with a wipe-off pen.

- proper nouns that name specific persons, places, things, or ideas—the *Dallas Cowboys*

dr. steven gary
st. stephen's hospital
durham, ca 38400

It's A Wrap!

Familiarize your students with the four basic sentence types and their ending punctuation marks with this star-studded lesson!

Skill: Classifying sentence types

Estimated Lesson Time: 45 minutes

Teacher Preparation:
1. Duplicate one copy of page 9 for each of your students.
2. Write an example of each of the four types of sentences on a different sentence strip.

Materials:
1 copy of page 9 for each student
1 sheet of 9" x 12" construction paper for each student
glue
scissors
4 sentence strips, each featuring an example of one of the four types of sentences

Background Information:
The four types of sentences are:
- *Declarative*—A declarative sentence makes a statement and ends with a period.
- *Interrogative*—An interrogative sentence asks a question and ends with a question mark.
- *Imperative*—An imperative sentence gives a command and ends with a period.
- *Exclamatory*—An exclamatory sentence shows strong emotion and ends with an exclamation point.

Introducing The Lesson:

Post the four sentence strips that feature the different types of sentences on the chalkboard, each strip in a separate column. Ask a student volunteer to read each of the four sentences aloud. Instruct your students to note any differences in purpose, content, and punctuation among the four sentences. Then identify each sentence as *declarative, interrogative, imperative,* or *exclamatory*.

Steps:

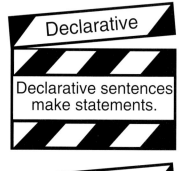

Declarative

Declarative sentences make statements.

1. Define each of the four sentence types (see the background information on page 7). Write the definitions under their appropriate columns on the board.

2. Together brainstorm situations in which each of the different types of sentences could be used. Point out that interrogative sentences are used to make inquiries, and that imperative sentences are used to give instructions. Explain that exclamatory sentences are used to show strong emotions or feelings, and that declarative sentences are used to make statements.

Interrogative

Interrogative sentences ask questions.

3. Ask students to give examples of each of the four types of sentences. Record these examples on the board in their appropriate columns. Review the punctuation mark used with each type of sentence.

4. Provide each child with a copy of page 9 and a sheet of 9" x 12" construction paper.

Imperative

Imperative sentences give commands.

5. Instruct each student to divide his construction paper into four equal columns. Then have the student cut out the four clapboards on page 9 and glue each one in a different column on his paper.

6. Next direct the student to cut out the megaphones on page 9, add the correct ending punctuation to each of the megaphones' sentences, and then glue the megaphones under the appropriate columns on his paper.

Exclamatory

Exclamatory sentences show emotion or surprise.

7. Then ask each student to write a sentence on each of the four remaining blank megaphones, one sentence for each type. Instruct the student to glue these megaphones under their correct columns as well.

8. Collect the students' papers, or check them together as a class review.

It's A Wrap!

Directions: Divide a sheet of construction paper into four columns. Cut out the four clapboards below; then glue one clapboard at the top of each column. Next cut out the megaphones. Determine which type of sentence is written on each megaphone and add the correct ending punctuation to it. Also write a different kind of sentence on each blank megaphone. Then glue each megaphone under its correct clapboard.

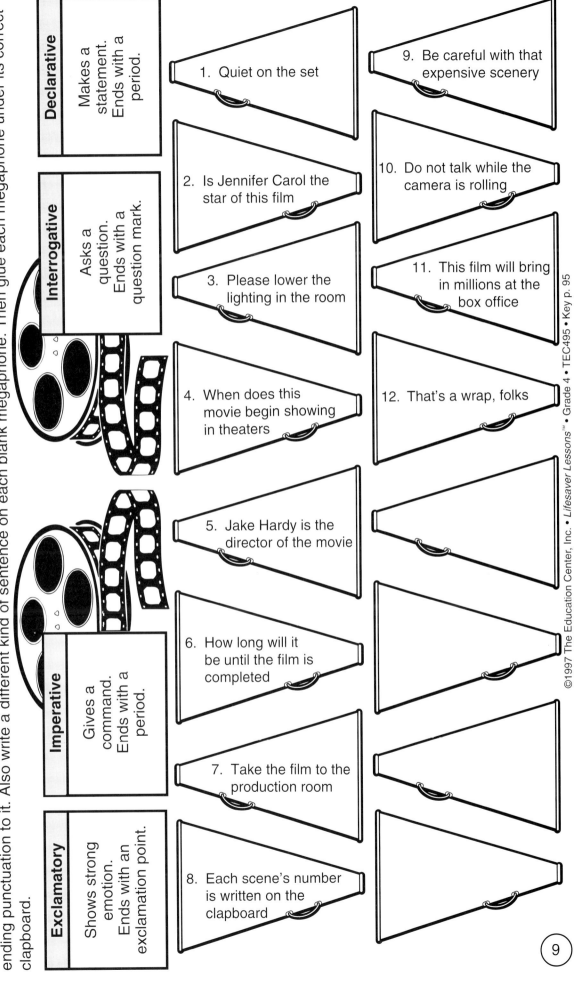

Declarative
Makes a statement. Ends with a period.

Interrogative
Asks a question. Ends with a question mark.

Imperative
Gives a command. Ends with a period.

Exclamatory
Shows strong emotion. Ends with an exclamation point.

1. Quiet on the set

2. Is Jennifer Carol the star of this film

3. Please lower the lighting in the room

4. When does this movie begin showing in theaters

5. Jake Hardy is the director of the movie

6. How long will it be until the film is completed

7. Take the film to the production room

8. Each scene's number is written on the clapboard

9. Be careful with that expensive scenery

10. Do not talk while the camera is rolling

11. This film will bring in millions at the box office

12. That's a wrap, folks

©1997 The Education Center, Inc. • *Lifesaver Lessons*™ • Grade 4 • TEC495 • Key p. 95

How To Extend The Lesson:

- Record the names of different animals on strips of paper—one for every two students in your class—and place the names inside a jar. Divide your students into pairs; then allow each pair to select a strip of paper from the jar. Without naming it, challenge each pair to write four sentences that describe the animal listed on their slip of paper. Require that each description consist of one declarative sentence, one interrogative sentence, one imperative sentence, and one exclamatory sentence. Afterward, have the pairs share their descriptions aloud and call on classmates to identify the animals they described.

- Divide your students into pairs. Give each pair a sheet of construction paper, scissors, glue, and a section of the newspaper. Instruct the pair to divide its construction paper into four equal sections, one section for each type of sentence. Have students cut out examples of each of the four kinds of sentences from the newspaper and glue them in the appropriate categories.

- Play a game to review interrogative sentences with your class. Divide your students into teams. Give each child an index card; then have him write an answer to any question on the card. For example, the student could write "It has whiskers, four legs, and meows." Collect the index cards and shuffle them; then select a card and read it aloud. Instruct each student to write a question that could result in the answer that you read aloud. Call on one member of each team to share his response. Give each team one point for an acceptable response. Continue play until all of the cards have been read.

- Challenge each student to alter the meaning of a given sentence by changing its ending punctuation. For example, the sentence below changes from a statement to an interrogative sentence when a question mark is substituted for the period. Direct each student to suggest a similar sentence in which the sentence's meaning changes significantly when its punctuation is altered.

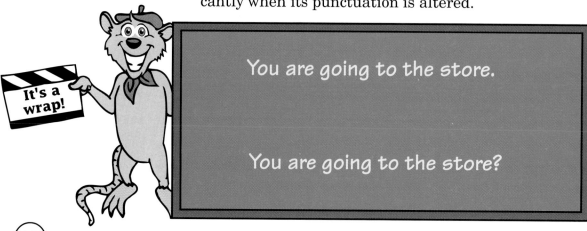

It's a wrap!

You are going to the store.

You are going to the store?

Name That Noun!

Make proper nouns become common sights with this picture-perfect lesson!

Skills: Identifying common and proper nouns; using nouns correctly

Estimated Lesson Time: 45 minutes

Teacher Preparation:

1. Duplicate a copy of page 13 for each student.
2. Divide the length of your chalkboard into eight sections.
3. Label these eight sections with the following common-noun headings: "person," "toy/game," "vehicle," "food," "city," "building," "business," and "date."

Materials:

old magazines
scissors
glue
masking tape
several sheets of same-colored construction paper for each team of four—a different color for each team
1 copy of page 13 for each student

Background Information:

A *common noun* is a word that names any ordinary person, animal, place, thing, or idea. For example: *lady, kitten, city, marble,* and *kindness.*

A *proper noun* is a word that names a very specific person, animal, place, or thing. For example: *Rosa Parks, Muffin, Oak Hollow Mall,* and *Carnival Cruise Lines*®. Proper nouns always begin with capital letters.

Introducing The Lesson:

Ask your students the following questions: "Is a Whopper® a hamburger?", "Is *The Best School Year Ever* a book?", and "Is Disney World® a place to visit?" Then guide your students through the steps below to help them identify and use common and proper nouns.

Steps:

1. Review the difference between common nouns and proper nouns (see page 11). Then challenge your students to name several common nouns and suggest proper nouns for them. For example: dog—Boomer.

2. Direct your students' attention to the labeled sections on your chalkboard. Have volunteers suggest examples of proper nouns for the common nouns that are labeled on the board. For example: building—Empire State Building.

3. Next divide your students into teams of four. Give each team a supply of magazines, scissors, glue, and masking tape. Also give each team several sheets of colored paper, giving a different color of paper to each team.

4. Instruct each team to find and cut out magazine pictures of proper nouns for each common-noun category on the board. Afterward direct each team to mount each picture on a cutout of colored paper that is slightly larger than the picture.

5. As the pictures are completed, direct each team to put a roll of tape on the back of each proper-noun picture and attach it to its corresponding common-noun section on the chalkboard. Declare the first team to find and tape a picture in every category on the board the winner!

6. If desired, display these pictures in a grid on a bulletin board with the same categories and title as shown.

7. Give students more practice with identifying common and proper nouns by assigning the reproducible on page 13.

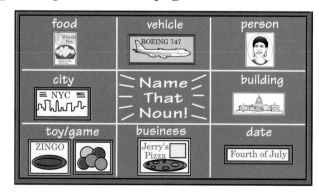

Name That Noun!

Directions: Underline all of the common nouns in each sentence below. Next draw a picture for each sentence in the box provided for it. Then rewrite each sentence by replacing all of the common nouns in it with proper nouns that match its picture.

Example: The **girl** went to the **city**. **Princess Meg** went to **Paris**.

1.

1. The pet ate the food.

   _____.

2. I got a toy on the holiday.

   _____.

2.

3.

3. The boy used soap to wash the car.

   _____.

4. The city is in a state.

   _____.

4.

5.

5. The president went to the store.

   _____.

Bonus Box: Write a story on the back of this sheet about one of the pictures above. Then reread your story, circling each common noun and underlining each proper noun that you used.

(13)

How To Extend The Lesson:

- Provide each student with a magazine picture of a very detailed scene. Instruct him to list the common nouns that he sees represented in this picture. Then have the student create a story about his picture, substituting proper nouns for common nouns whenever possible.

- Divide your class into small groups; then have each group sit in a circle. Give each group a pencil and an 8 1/2" x 11" sheet of paper. Direct one member of each group to divide his group's paper into two columns—one for common nouns and the other for proper nouns. Announce a category, such as "transportation." Allow each group one minute to pass around its paper and pencil and list as many nouns for each column as possible. Explain that all the nouns that are listed must relate to the announced category. When time is up, have each group in turn read its list aloud. Declare the group with the most correctly placed nouns the winner. Continue play by announcing a new category.

- Write seven common nouns and seven proper nouns, each on a separate 3" x 5" index card. Afterward place the cards in an open container. Play some music, stopping it periodically. Have students pass around a spongy, soft ball while the music is playing. When you stop the music, instruct the student who is holding the ball to draw a card from the container, announce the noun to the class, and then classify that noun as common or proper.

Common Nouns	Proper Nouns
country	France
lake	Lake Superior
hero	Paul Bunyan
day	Saturday
scientist	Isaac Newton
man	Paul Newsome
county	Guilford County
event	All-Star Weekend
explorer	Marco Polo
organization	Red Cross
inventor	Benjamin Franklin
mountain	Mt. Mitchell
holiday	Valentine's Day
state	Florida
woman	Caroline Thompson
continent	Asia
leader	President Clinton
planet	Earth
river	Mississippi River
city	New Orleans

- Instruct each student to copy the following 20 common nouns on his paper in a column: *country, lake, hero, day, scientist, man, county, event, explorer, organization, inventor, mountain, holiday, state, woman, continent, leader, planet, river,* and *city.* Then have the student use his textbooks or other nonfiction books to find one or more proper nouns that match each common noun.

Action Heroes

*Move over, Superman® and Wonder Woman®!
Make way for action-verb superheroes!*

Skills: Identifying action verbs; using action verbs; creating an imaginary character

Estimated Lesson Time: 45 minutes

Teacher Preparation:
Duplicate a copy of page 17 for each student.

Materials:
1 copy of page 17 for each student
1 sheet of loose-leaf paper for each student
pencils
crayons

Background Information:
A verb that shows action is called an *action verb*. An action verb specifically identifies what the subject is doing—physically or mentally. For example: Jeff *watched* the basketball game, while Susan *wondered* what time it was.

Introducing The Lesson:

Set the stage for this action-packed lesson by having students name their favorite action heroes. As each student shares the name of his favorite hero, write that character's name on the board; then have that student briefly describe the actions that are usually associated with that particular superhero. Then guide your students through the following steps that challenge them to create their own action heroes.

Steps:

1. Give each student a copy of page 17. Direct him to complete the reproducible according to its directions.

2. Afterward have students share which 15 action verbs should have been circled at the bottom of the reproducible. Write these words on the chalkboard for clarification.

3. Next pair students and have them position their action-hero pictures on top of their desks so that the pictures are visible to both partners.

4. Instruct each student to write a short story about a time when his action hero meets his partner's hero. Explain that each story should contain as many of the action verbs listed on the chalkboard as possible.

5. After the stories have been written, direct the partners to exchange papers. Have each student read his partner's story and circle the action verbs it contains. Collect your students' stories and display them along with their super action-hero characters on a wall or bulletin board.

Some Action Verbs

swim	think	scramble
climb	listen	scamper
throw	dream	hustle
breathe	laugh	sleep

Star-Studded Action Heroes

Directions: Design your own action hero inside the star-framed box below. Make your character as large and colorful as possible. Then look at the list of words at the bottom of this sheet. Circle the 15 words that are action verbs. Then choose five of the circled words. Use each chosen word in a different sentence on the back of this sheet.

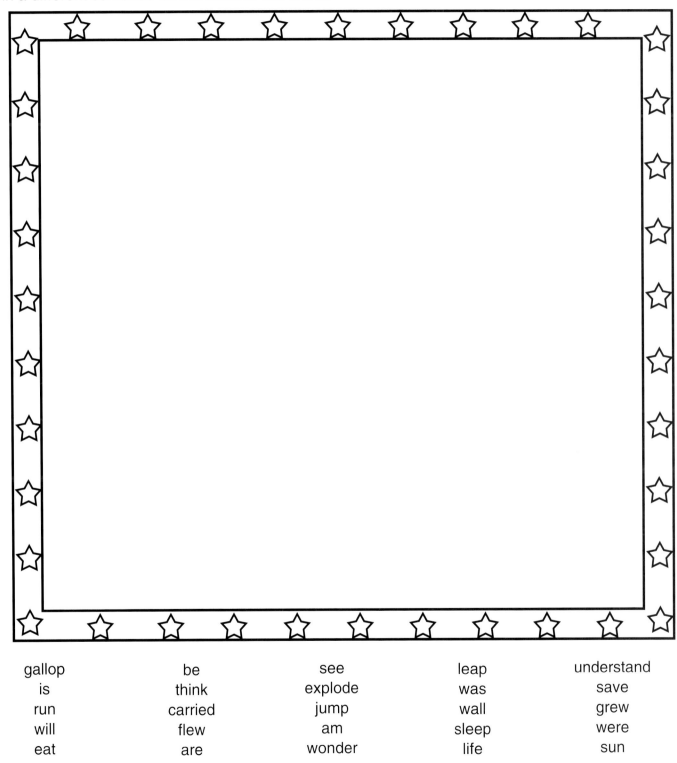

gallop	be	see	leap	understand
is	think	explode	was	save
run	carried	jump	wall	grew
will	flew	am	sleep	were
eat	are	wonder	life	sun

Bonus Box: Think of a person you know who—in your opinion—is a hero. Write a story about spending a day with this real-life hero and the good deeds that he/she does.

©1997 The Education Center, Inc. • *Lifesaver Lessons*™ • Grade 4 • TEC495 • Key p. 95

How To Extend The Lesson:

- For a quick transition between subjects that gets everyone moving, act out action verbs! Simply have your students stand next to their desks and pantomime action verbs of their choice whenever they hear you say, "Be a verb!" For example, one student might run in place while another hops up and down. After 15 seconds, expect everyone to be refreshed and ready to work again!

- Involve your students in making personal action-verb dictionaries. Together, brainstorm a list of 15–20 unusual and vivid verbs. Next have each student choose any ten of these words; then direct her to write each word on a different sheet of 8" x 11" white paper. Also on each sheet, instruct the student to write the definition of that word and use it in a sentence. Then direct her to draw—or look in a magazine for—a picture that illustrates that action verb. When her pages are complete, have the student compile them into a booklet titled "Action-Verb Dictionary" that she can keep at her desk.

- Provide students with a visible and ready resource for action-specific verbs. Have each student remove one shoe and trace its outline on a piece of construction paper. After the shoe shapes have been cut out, brainstorm a list of action verbs with your students. Record their suggestions on the board; then assign one verb to each student. Have him write the assigned verb on his cutout with a crayon or marker. Staple the shoe cutouts on a bulletin board titled "Step Into Action!" Suggest that your students refer to the board whenever they need specific verbs for their writing.

Dreaming Up Subjects And Predicates

Recognizing subjects and predicates will bring sweet dreams with the help of this fun activity!

Skills: Recognizing subjects and predicates; writing sentences with complete subjects and predicates

Estimated Lesson Time: 45 minutes

Teacher Preparation:
Duplicate one copy of page 21 for each student.

Materials:
1 copy of page 21 for each student

Background Information:
Every sentence is made up of two parts—the subject and the predicate. The *complete subject* includes all the words that tell who or what the sentence is about. The *complete predicate* includes all the words that tell what the subject of the sentence is or does.

Recognizing subjects and predicates (19)

Introducing The Lesson:

Begin the lesson by drawing a simple puzzle—with one of its pieces missing—on your chalkboard as shown. Ask your students if they notice anything strange about the puzzle. After your students point out that one piece of the puzzle is missing, complete the drawing by adding its missing piece. Relate the puzzle with its missing piece to a sentence that is missing one of its parts: either its subject or its predicate. Explain that just as the puzzle needed all of its pieces to be complete, a sentence needs its two parts—the subject and the predicate—to be complete.

Steps:

1. Define *subject* and *predicate* for your students, and discuss the meaning of each one (see "Background Information" on page 19).

2. Choose one of the sentences from the list below and write it on the board. Have a student come to the board and circle the complete subject of this sentence. Check this student's answer for accuracy (the complete subject is italicized). Afterward point out that all of the remaining words make up the complete predicate. Repeat this procedure with the remaining sentences.
   - *Jennifer* likes to sleep with her teddy bear.
   - *The long ride home* made everyone very tired.
   - *My cats, Penny and Tuffy,* like to sleep at the foot of my bed.
   - *My mother* says you should get at least eight hours of sleep each night.
   - *Sarah and Jackie's bedtime* is at ten o'clock.
   - *Mike* usually falls asleep in front of the television.
   - *A lack of sleep* often leaves you feeling tired.
   - When my friends spend the night, *we* stay up until midnight!

3. Give each student a copy of page 21. Have each student complete this sheet according to its directions.

Dreaming Of Subjects And Predicates

Subject—tells who or what the sentence is about
Predicate—tells what the subject is or does

ZZZZz

Directions: Read each sentence below. Decide whether the underlined part is a complete subject or a complete predicate. Then write the underlined part in the appropriate cloud.

1. My little sister and I <u>go to bed at 9:00 P.M.</u>
2. The quilt that my grandmother made <u>keeps me warm.</u>
3. <u>My little sister and I</u> share a room.
4. <u>Scrappy, the family dog,</u> often sleeps with us.
5. <u>The streetlight</u> shines brightly outside our bedroom window at night.
6. Our mom and dad <u>tell us bedtime stories each night.</u>
7. <u>Carrie</u> is afraid of the dark.
8. Sometimes <u>I</u> can't sleep because Scrappy snores!
9. <u>The alarm clock</u> wakes us up every morning at 7:00 A.M.
10. Our mother and father's room <u>is down the hall from ours.</u>
11. <u>Aunt Sharon</u> crocheted a pretty afghan for Carrie's bed.
12. In the summer, <u>my bedtime</u> is later than it is during the school year.

SUBJECTS

PREDICATES

Bonus Box: Write five sentences on the back of this sheet. In each sentence, circle the complete subject and underline the complete predicate.

(21)

©1997 The Education Center, Inc. • *Lifesaver Lessons*™ • Grade 4 • TEC495 • Key p. 95

How To Extend The Lesson:

- Have each student write five descriptive sentences about himself on a sheet of paper. In these sentences, direct the student to refer to himself in the third person. Collect your students' papers. Choose one sentence about each student; then write each sentence on a different sentence strip. Cut each strip apart so that the complete subject is on one half of the sentence strip and the complete predicate is on the other half. Divide a bulletin board in half. Write "Complete Subjects" on the left side of the board and "Complete Predicates" on the right. Shuffle the subject and predicate strips; then read the strips aloud one at a time. Call on a different student each time to classify the announced group of words as a complete subject or a complete predicate. Afterward have that student attach that sentence-strip part underneath the appropriate heading with masking tape.

- Select a picture book that has only two to three sentences on every page. Then have each student divide a sheet of loose-leaf paper into two columns titled "Complete Subjects" and "Complete Predicates." As you read the book aloud, choose one sentence from each page to write on the board. Then have each student write that sentence's complete subject and predicate under the appropriate headings on her paper.

- Divide your class into groups of six for a subject and predicate game. Write several sentences on your chalkboard, enough so that each group has a different sentence. Assign each group member one of the tasks below. Then assign each group a different sentence. Give each group two minutes to complete all six tasks for its assigned sentence. When time is up, ask each group's reporter to come to the front of the room, in turn, and share the group's answers. If the answers are correct, reward that group with one point. After all of the groups have reported, assign each group a different sentence so that play can continue. After the groups have worked with all the assigned sentences, declare the group with the most points the winner.

1. Copy the sentence on paper.
2. Underline the complete subject.
3. Circle the complete predicate.

4. Draw a box around the simple subject.
5. Underline the simple predicate twice.
6. Be the reporter.

My favorite bedtime story lasts about 15 minutes.

Cutting It Short!

Brief your students on abbreviations with this fun-filled lesson.

Skill: Writing abbreviations in party invitations and addresses

Estimated Lesson Time: 45 minutes

Teacher Preparation:

Duplicate one copy of the reproducible on page 25 for each student.

Materials:

1 copy of page 25 for each student
one 8 1/2" x 11" sheet of white drawing paper for each student
crayons or colored pencils

Background Information:

Abbreviations are shortened forms of words. A period follows most abbreviations. Abbreviations are always used with other words or names. They are never used as words by themselves. For example, "The Coxes live on a beautiful *street*" (no abbreviation). But "Deliver this to 45 Market *St.*" Some common abbreviations are:

- *Days of the week:* Mon.; Tues.; Wed.; Thurs.; Fri.; Sat.; Sun.
- *Months of the year:* Jan.; Feb.; Mar.; Apr.; Aug.; Sept.; Oct.; Nov.; Dec.
- *Times of day:* A.M. and P.M.
- *Street addresses:* St.; Blvd.; Rd.; Dr.; Ave.; Rt.
- *States:* TN, VA (postal abbreviations use all capital letters and no periods)

Introducing The Lesson:

Write your school's address on the chalkboard without using any abbreviations. Then ask your students to explain how to rewrite this address using abbreviations.

Steps:

1. Explain to your students that abbreviations are shortened forms of words. Write the two sample sentences included in the background information on page 23 on the board. Refer to these sentences to show that an abbreviation is used only when it is accompanied by another word.

2. Next write the abbreviations from page 23 on the chalkboard. Point out that, except for postal abbreviations, each abbreviation begins with a capital letter and is followed by a period.

3. Give each child an 8 1/2" x 11" sheet of drawing paper and crayons or colored pencils. Then have her fold her paper in half so that it resembles a greeting card.

4. Direct each child to write an invitation to a birthday party inside her folded paper. Explain that this invitation should include the date, time, and location of the party, plus a date by which to respond as shown. Require that each line of the invitation include at least one abbreviation.

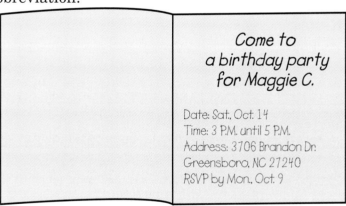

Come to
a birthday party
for Maggie C.

Date: Sat., Oct. 14
Time: 3 P.M. until 5 P.M.
Address: 3706 Brandon Dr.
Greensboro, NC 27240
RSVP by Mon., Oct. 9

5. Instruct your students to use crayons or colored pencils to decorate the front covers of their invitations. Then display these invitations on a bulletin board titled "You're Invited!"

6. Provide additional practice with abbreviations by having each student complete the reproducible on page 25.

Addresses Please!

Even make-believe characters need addresses! Make up an address for each character on the lines of each envelope below. Make sure that each line of the address includes at least one abbreviation and relates to the character named on the envelope (see the example).

Bob B. Socks
117 Foot St.
Shoe, NY 00117

1.

Mr. Big B. Wolf

_____

_____

2.

Mr. Frank N. Stein

_____

_____

3.

Mr. Tom Turkey

_____

_____

4.

Mr. San T. Claws

_____

_____

5.

Ms. Tooth Fairy

_____

_____

6.

Mr. E. Ster Bunny

_____

_____

Bonus Box: Draw and color a special stamp on each envelope above. Design each stamp so that it represents that particular character.

©1997 The Education Center, Inc. • *Lifesaver Lessons*™ • Grade 4 • TEC495

How To Extend The Lesson:

- Record a list of favorite book characters brainstormed by your class on the chalkboard. Then instruct each student to choose five characters from this list and create a make-believe address for each one. Remind each student to include an abbreviation on each line of the address and to relate the address to each character in a creative way. Give each student a business-sized envelope on which to record his favorite fictitious address. Afterward instruct each student to design a stamp for his envelope and decorate it so that it represents that character. Then staple your students' envelopes to a bulletin board titled "The Literary White Pages."

- Divide your class into groups of three or four students. Give each group a large sheet of bulletin-board paper and crayons or colored pencils. Assign each group a different section of an imaginary town to draw on its paper. Require that labels with abbreviations for streets, buildings, and landmarks be included in each section. Display these bulletin-board sheets side by side as a mural in the main hallway of your school under the heading "Shortcuts Around Town."

- As a class, brainstorm a list of abbreviations used in recipes. List your students' responses on the chalkboard. Give each student an index or recipe card; then challenge her to use at least five of these abbreviations to create a recipe for "Friendship Stew." Post your students' recipe cards on a bulletin board with the same title.

Goin' Ape Over Apostrophes!

Familiarize your students with the correct usage of apostrophes with this "ape-peeling" lesson.

Skill: Using apostrophes to form plurals, to show possession, and to show the omission of letters or numbers in a word or numeral

Estimated Lesson Time: 45 minutes

Teacher Preparation:
Duplicate one copy of page 29 for each student.

Materials:
1 copy of the current class novel or story for each student
1 copy of page 29 for each student
crayons
scissors
masking tape

Background Information:
Apostrophes are used to show possession.
- The possessive form of a singular noun is formed by adding an apostrophe and an *s* to the noun. For example: The man crossed the *snake's* path.
- The possessive form of a plural noun ending in *s* is formed by adding an apostrophe. For example: The *boys'* basketball team won the championship. However, if the plural of the noun does not end in *s*, the possessive is formed by adding an apostrophe and an *s*. For example: The *children's* library is open.

Apostrophes are used to form plurals.
- An apostrophe and an *s* can be added to form the plural of a number, letter, or sign. For example: The Oakland *A's* are a great baseball team.

Apostrophes are used to show that letters or numbers have been left out.
- An apostrophe in a contraction shows that one or more letters have been omitted. For example, *shouldn't* = should not, *they're* = they are.
- Apostrophes also show that letters or numbers have been left out of words or numerals. For example: Bill said, "John is *goin'* to graduate with the class of *'97.*"

Introducing The Lesson:

Challenge your students to search through their current class novel or story to find ten words, letters, or numbers that use apostrophes and then write these items on paper. As your students work, make three columns on your chalkboard and label them "Forming Possessives," "Forming Plurals," and "In Place Of Letters/Numbers."

Steps:

1. Have your students share their findings with the class. As they do, record several of their responses as examples under each heading on the board. Also discuss the corresponding rule for using each apostrophe (see page 27). Instruct each student to keep his word list for use later in the lesson.

2. Give each student a copy of page 29, have him complete the bottom portion of the sheet as independent practice, and then check the sheet together as a class.

3. Afterward give each student a pair of scissors and crayons. Direct each student to choose one word from the word list he created earlier and record it on his banana at the top of his reproducible with a dark crayon.

4. Have the student color and cut out the banana. Meanwhile erase the examples contributed by your students from the chalkboard, leaving the columns and headings intact.

5. Give each child a three-inch strip of masking tape; then instruct him to roll this strip and place it on the back of his banana cutout.

6. As a class review, have each student, in turn, come to the board and position his banana in its appropriate column. As he does, review the rule that the word on the banana represents.

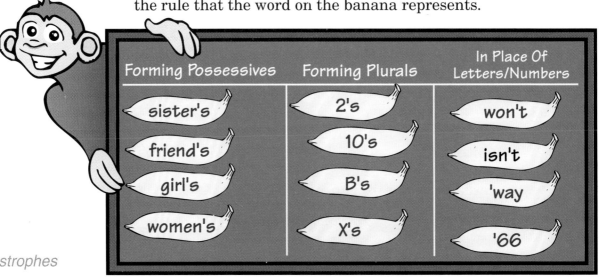

Forming Possessives	Forming Plurals	In Place Of Letters/Numbers
sister's	2's	won't
friend's	10's	isn't
girl's	B's	'way
women's	X's	'66

©1997 The Education Center, Inc. • *Lifesaver Lessons*™ • Grade 4 • TEC495

Name _____

Apostrophes

Goin' Ape Over Apostrophes!

Directions: Read each sentence below. Then insert an apostrophe where it is needed in each underlined word.

1. Jane <u>Goodalls</u> work to ensure the survival of chimpanzees in the wild has made her famous.

2. Beginning in <u>60</u>, Jane Goodall began observing chimpanzees at close range.

3. She won the <u>chimpanzees</u> trust by having daily contact with them.

4. Because apes only live in the tropical areas of Africa and Asia, they <u>cant</u> be found in the North American wild.

5. The orangutan enjoys <u>swingin</u> from tree branches.

6. All four of an <u>apes</u> limbs are used to support its body weight.

7. A <u>gorillas</u> diet consists mainly of wild celery and bamboo shoots.

8. Monkeys <u>arent</u> the same as apes.

9. <u>Asias</u> tropical forests are the <u>gibbons</u> homes.

10. If male <u>gorillas</u> backs are covered with white or silver hair, they are called silverbacks.

Bonus Box: On the back of this sheet, write a paragraph that contains at least ten words with apostrophes.

How To Extend The Lesson:

• Have your students create a contraction card game based on the correct usage of apostrophes. Pair your students; then give each pair a set of 20 blank index cards. Instruct the partners to think of ten different contractions. Then have them program the cards with their contractions by writing a contraction on one card and the two words that make up that contraction on another card. For example, if *shouldn't* is written on one card, its mate will have *should not* written on it. After the students in each pair have programmed their cards, have them shuffle the set of cards and place them inside an envelope. Instruct each pair of students to exchange their game cards with another pair before playing a matching game.

• Challenge your students to look through old magazines and newspapers for words or numbers that contain apostrophes. Afterward instruct the students to cut out these examples and categorize them according to how the apostrophe is used in each word. Then have the students glue the cut-out words and numbers onto sheets of construction paper by categories to display in your room.

• Put a fun spin on apostrophes with this activity. Stock a classroom learning center with elbow macaroni noodles, glue, sentence strips, and colored markers. When visiting the center, instruct each student to use a marker to write a sentence on a sentence strip that has one or more words requiring an apostrophe. Suggest that the student glue an elbow macaroni in each place where an apostrophe is needed in the sentence. Then display each student's sentence strip in the center for others to enjoy.

The Nuts And Bolts Of Narrative Writing

Help your students get a grip on narrative writing with this lesson.

Skill: Identifying the elements of a narrative

Estimated Lesson Time: 45 minutes–1 hour

Teacher Preparation:
1. Duplicate one copy of page 33 for each student.
2. Select a short narrative from your school library to read aloud.

Materials:
1 copy of page 33 for each student
a short narrative story to read aloud
crayons

The Elements Of A Narrative Are:

Characters
Setting
Plot

Background Information:
The purpose of narrative writing—to tell a story about a particular experience—is different from other types of writing. In descriptive writing, very specific details are used to describe a person, place, thing, or an event. In persuasive writing, the writer expresses an opinion. In expository writing, the writer gives an explanation about something.

Because narrative writing is often organized in chronological order, sequencing words—such as *first, then, next,* and *finally*—are commonly used to order its events. The elements of a narrative are:
- *Characters*—the people or animals in a story
- *Setting*—where and when the story takes place
- *Plot*—how a character's problem gets solved

Introducing The Lesson:

Point out to students that storytelling has been a popular form of entertainment since the beginning of time. Explain that people enjoy telling about their own personal adventures and the experiences of others as well. Instruct your students to listen carefully as you read aloud a short narrative so that they will be able to answer your questions afterward.

Steps:

1. After reading, review the elements of a narrative—characters, setting, and plot. Discuss the meaning of each component (see page 31); then ask your students to identify each of these elements in the story you read aloud.

2. Explain that a narrative shares an experience by using details that tell *who, what, when, where, why,* and *how.*

3. Have your students describe how narrative writing differs from descriptive, expository, and persuasive forms of writing (see page 31).

4. Provide each student with crayons and a copy of page 33.

5. Instruct each student to follow the directions on the sheet to write a narrative, reminding her to use colorful details to keep the reader's interest.

6. Display your students' narratives on a wall or bulletin board.

Principal For A Day

Directions: Imagine that you have been chosen to act as the principal of your school for a day! Write a narrative that tells about your special day on the lines below. Be sure to include plenty of details about your characters, setting, and plot. When you finish your narrative, color the border around it to make an attractive frame for your story.

_____

_____

_____

_____

_____

_____

_____

_____

_____

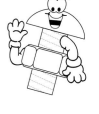

_____

_____

_____

_____

_____

©1997 The Education Center, Inc. • *Lifesaver Lessons*™ • Grade 4 • TEC495

How To Extend The Lesson:

- List several vocabulary words from your current read-aloud on the board. Instruct each student to begin writing a narrative that uses some of the words from this list. After three minutes, say, "Pass," and direct each student to give his paper to the student on his left. Instruct each student to read what is written on the paper he receives. Then allow him to add to the story on that paper, continuing to use the vocabulary words from the board. Have your students continue to write and pass the narratives four more times. Before making the last pass, announce that it is the last one and that students will have exactly three minutes to conclude their stories. Then have volunteers share some of the stories.

- Challenge each student to assume the identity of a historical figure from your current social studies unit. Then direct the student to write a narrative that details an important event in the life of this individual. For example, if a student selects Paul Revere, suggest that he write about Revere's famous midnight ride. Also suggest that the student make a prop—such as a hat to wear or a lantern to carry—and use it when he shares his narrative aloud with the class.

- Provide each student with three index cards. Instruct the student to write the name of a character on the first card, a setting on the second card, and a problem on the third card. Afterward collect the cards from your students and sort them into three categories. Then shuffle the cards and redistribute them so that each student has a card from all three categories. Instruct the student to write a narrative that incorporates all three of the elements listed on his cards. Remind your students to supply interesting details that will make their stories fun to read.

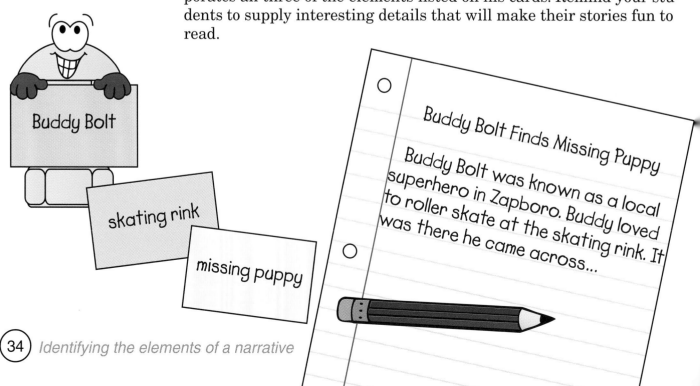

Identifying the elements of a narrative

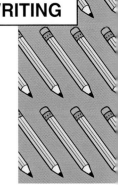

Destination: Anywhere!

*Help your students navigate the expository-writing process
with this fun lesson on writing directions.*

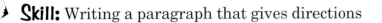

Skill: Writing a paragraph that gives directions

Estimated Lesson Time: 45 minutes

Teacher Preparation:

1. Duplicate one copy of page 37 for each student.
2. Write a paragraph that explains how to walk from your classroom to the school cafeteria on a blank transparency. Make sure this paragraph contains one or more transition words (see "Background Information" below).

Materials:

1 transparency
1 copy of page 37 for each student
overhead projector

Background Information:

An *expository* paragraph gives information about a topic. This type of paragraph explains ideas, gives directions, or spells out how something is done. Transition words—such as *first, second,* and *next*—guide the reader through the explanation.

Introducing The Lesson:

Display the transparency that you created on an overhead projector; then read the paragraph on it aloud to your class. Ask your students, "What is the purpose of this paragraph?" *(It explains how to get from the classroom to the cafeteria.)*

Steps:

1. Explain the purpose of an expository paragraph (see page 35).

2. Refer to the transparency to point out the transition words that were used to guide the reader through the explanation (see page 35).

3. Give each student a copy of the reproducible on page 37. Instruct each student to choose two of the locations printed in bold type on the map. Explain that one location should be used as a starting point and the other as a destination. Then have him write an expository paragraph that tells how to get from his point of origin to his destination by using cardinal directions, and mentioning landmarks and names of specific streets. Remind him to include transition words.

4. Pair your students; then have each child exchange papers with his partner. Direct each student to refer to his map as he reads his partner's paper. If his partner's directions are inaccurate or unclear, have him return the paper to its author for corrections.

5. Share several well-written paragraphs with the class to reinforce the elements of an expository paragraph.

> First, follow the dirt path that runs west toward Buzzard's Junction. Go left...

How To Get To Baldhead Mountain

First, follow the dirt path that runs west toward Buzzard's Junction. Go left at the second fork in the path. Continue until you come to a large gray rock about ten feet in diameter that has the words "Gilbert was here!" on it. Then look to your right to see the path that leads up the mountain.

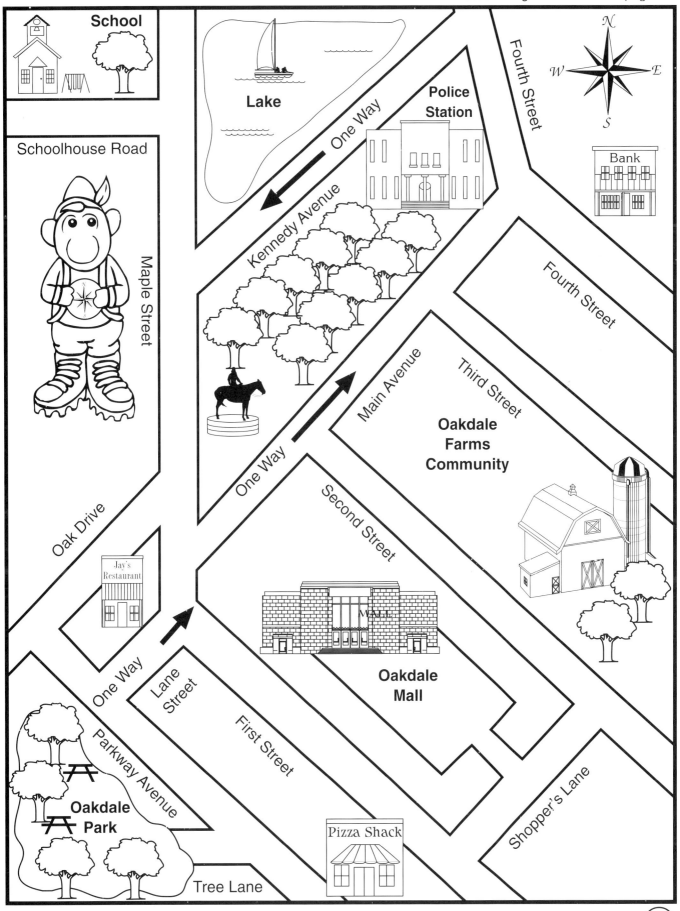

©1997 The Education Center, Inc. • *Lifesaver Lessons*™ • Grade 4 • TEC495

How To Extend The Lesson:

- Display the collection of expository-writing topics below on chart paper in a writing center.

Explain How To...

brush your teeth
wash the car
make a pizza
care for your pet
clean your room
study for a test
write a research report
bake a cake
decorate a Christmas tree
make an ice-cream sundae
play soccer, baseball, football, or another sport
care for a garden
ride a bicycle
divide 425 by 5
play a particular board game or card game
make your bed
wash your dog
wrap a present
get ready for trick-or-treating on Halloween
multiply 632 by 8
tie your shoes
use a compass to draw a circle with a diameter of 6 cm

- Give each student crayons and a sheet of drawing paper for creating a simple picture. As he draws, instruct him to write down his steps one by one in a logical and sequential order on loose-leaf paper. When he finishes his drawing, have him turn it facedown on his desk. Then pair your students and give each child a second sheet of drawing paper. Direct each student to exchange his written directions with his partner and follow his partner's written directions to draw a picture. When these drawings are complete, have each partner compare his drawing with the original to see how successfully the directions were written.

Dare To Compare

Equip your students with the skills they need for comparative writing.

Skill: Writing to compare two items

Estimated Lesson Time: 60 minutes

Teacher Preparation:
Duplicate one copy of page 41 for each student.

Materials:
1 copy of page 41 for each student
2 shoes, each a different type

How are we alike?

Background Information:
    Comparative writing involves comparing two items based upon their common characteristics. To understand the similarities between two objects, a chart, table, or Venn diagram can be used to help organize and identify similar attributes.
    Specific words and phrases often indicate when items are being compared. For example, *in the same way, also, likewise, like, as,* and *similarly.*

Introducing The Lesson:

Display two different shoes in the front of your classroom. Ask your students to study the two shoes carefully. Then guide your students through the steps below to help them compare the two shoes and list their similarities.

Steps:

1. Point out that it is necessary to look for common characteristics when comparing two items. Explain how important it is to note specific and accurate details about each item when making a comparison. Explain further that because a Venn diagram organizes information by its similarities and differences, it is a useful tool for comparing objects.

2. Draw a Venn diagram on the board. Write the name of one of the shoes in the left circle and the name of the second shoe in the right circle. Label the overlapping section of the circles "How the shoes are alike."

3. Ask your students to describe each shoe. As they do, list your students' responses inside the appropriate circles. Afterward point out the shoes' shared attributes that are listed in the overlapping section.

4. Have your students compare another pair of items—such as a basketball and a football, a pencil and a pen, or a car and a skateboard.

5. Review common words and phrases that are used to make comparisons (see the list on page 39).

6. Pair your students; then give each student a copy of page 41.

7. Instruct each student to follow the directions on the reproducible to compare herself to her partner.

8. Collect your students' comparisons.

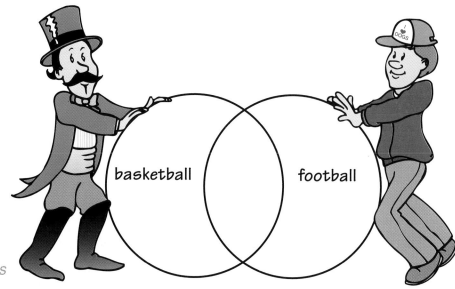

Dare To Compare

Directions: Write your name and the name of a classmate in the chart below. Interview the other student to find out how the two of you are alike and different in each area listed on the chart. Record your findings; then use that information to write a paragraph that tells about your similarities in the top half of the back of this sheet.

Name		
Age		
Birthday		
Favorite Color		
Favorite Foods		
Favorite Subject		
Pets		
Hobbies		
Family		
Career Plans		

Bonus Box: Write a paragraph that tells about the *differences* between you and your partner in the bottom half of the back of this sheet.

©1997 The Education Center, Inc. • *Lifesaver Lessons*™ • Grade 4 • TEC495

How To Extend The Lesson:

- Have each student use a Venn diagram to compare two of the characters from your current read-aloud. Remind your students to include details about the characters' appearances, personalities, likes, dislikes, problems, families, etc. Afterward instruct students to write about the similarities in a paragraph.

- Display a high-heeled shoe and a hiking boot. Challenge pairs of students to work together to write a conversation that might occur between these two shoes. Have the pairs pretend that the two shoes meet on a street and talk with each other. Require that all of the conversations focus on the differences between the two shoes. Suggest that your students incorporate details about the shoes' likes, dislikes, hobbies, and occupations within the context of their conversations.

- Read aloud a short story about the customs and traditions that are practiced in a specific foreign country. Then have each student write a paragraph that compares the customs of that country with those of the United States. Post your students' paragraphs on a bulletin board so that they surround a world map pinpointing the locations of the two featured countries.

France and the United States have many holidays in common. Some of the holidays celebrated in both countries are New Year's Day, Easter, April Fool's Day, May Day, and Christmas.

Taking Care Of Business

Help your students get down to business by writing effective business letters.

Skill: Writing a business letter

Estimated Lesson Time: 45 minutes

Teacher Preparation:
1. Duplicate one copy of page 45 for each student.
2. Make two transparencies: one friendly letter and one business letter.

Materials:
overhead transparencies: one friendly letter and one
    business letter
1 copy of page 45 for each student
1 sheet of loose-leaf paper for
    each student
1 stamped business envelope for
    each student
overhead projector

Sally Henderson
3801 Burba Road
New Haven, KY 40051

Arizona Office Of Tourism
1100 W. Washington St.
Phoenix, AZ 85007

Background Information:
Business letters are more formal and businesslike than friendly letters. They usually focus on one subject area or concern and have six main parts: the *heading*, the *inside address*, the *salutation*, the *body*, the *closing*, and the *signature*.
- *Heading*—the sender's address and the date, positioned at the left margin
- *Inside Address*—the name and address of the party to whom you are writing, located at the left margin below the heading
- *Salutation*—a greeting, positioned at the left margin on the second line after the inside address; followed by a colon
- *Body*—the main part of the letter, beginning two lines below the salutation with no indentation; double-spacing between paragraphs
- *Closing*—an ending phrase located two spaces below the body at the left margin, followed by a comma; first word capitalized
- *Signature*—the writer's name, positioned below the closing; if typewritten, four lines below the closing to allow space for signing

Introducing The Lesson:

Your students have probably written friendly letters at some point in time, but have they ever written business letters? Present a scenario that gives your students an understanding of when or why a business letter should be sent instead of a friendly letter. For example, pretend that your family is planning a trip to another state. Show your students a transparency of a letter to a friend sharing your optimism about the upcoming trip. Then show a transparency of a letter to a travel bureau requesting information about sites to visit in that state on your trip.

Steps:

1. Have your students point out the similarities and differences between a friendly letter and a business letter. Write their responses on the board in two columns, one labeled "Similarities" and the other labeled "Differences."

2. Give each student a copy of page 45 so that he can refer to the sample letter in the middle of the sheet as you introduce the parts of a business letter. Then label these respective letter parts on the transparency of the business letter that you shared with the class. Point out the number of parts in a business letter (six) and discuss the purpose and position of each part (see page 43).

3. Have each student select one of the organizations on page 45. Then instruct him to draft a letter to his chosen organization, following the correct business-letter format.

4. Afterward direct each student to exchange his letter with another student for peer editing. After each student edits his classmate's letter, instruct him to return the letter to its owner. Have each student make any necessary revisions to his letter and write his final copy on loose-leaf paper. Meanwhile, distribute a stamped business envelope to each student.

5. Demonstrate how to fold a business letter and also how to address a business envelope. Then have each student do the same with his letter and envelope.

6. Mail the students' letters; then post the responses as they are received.

Andrew Newton
3801 Burba Road
New Haven, KY 40051

Arizona Office Of Tourism
1100 W. Washington St.
Phoenix, AZ 85007

Getting Down To Business

Directions: Look at the six parts of a business letter labeled on the sample letter below. Next select one of the addresses that surround the letter. Write a letter to that organization requesting a map and travel information about that state. Use the sample letter as a guide for writing your business letter.

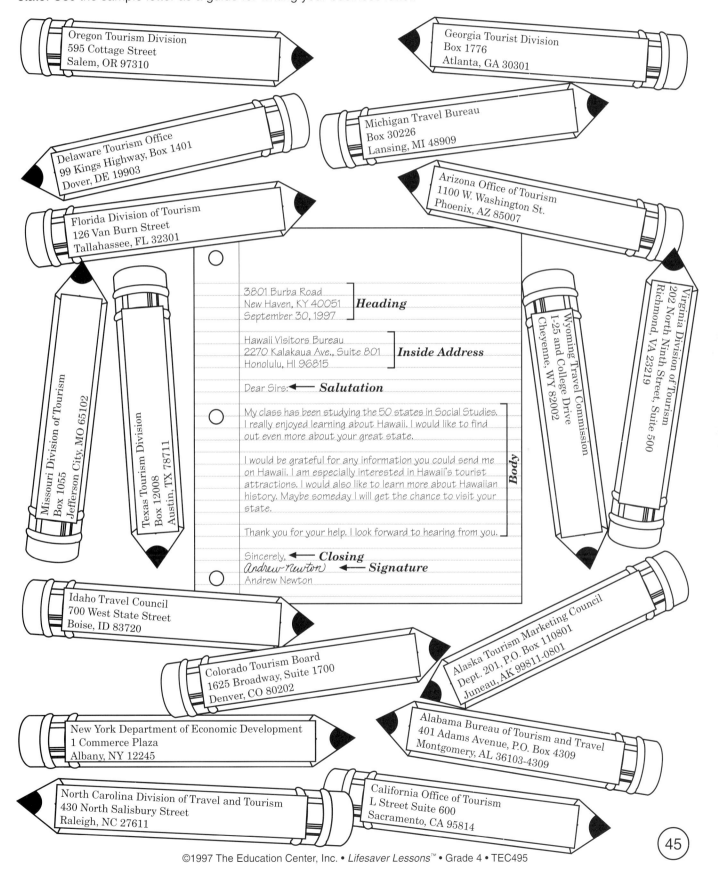

Oregon Tourism Division
595 Cottage Street
Salem, OR 97310

Georgia Tourist Division
Box 1776
Atlanta, GA 30301

Delaware Tourism Office
99 Kings Highway, Box 1401
Dover, DE 19903

Michigan Travel Bureau
Box 30226
Lansing, MI 48909

Florida Division of Tourism
126 Van Burn Street
Tallahassee, FL 32301

Arizona Office of Tourism
1100 W. Washington St.
Phoenix, AZ 85007

Missouri Division of Tourism
Box 1055
Jefferson City, MO 6502

Texas Tourism Division
Box 12008
Austin, TX 78711

Wyoming Travel Commission
I-25 and College Drive
Cheyenne, WY 82002

Virginia Division of Tourism
202 North Ninth Street,
Richmond, VA 23219
Suite 500

3801 Burba Road
New Haven, KY 40051
September 30, 1997 **Heading**

Hawaii Visitors Bureau
2270 Kalakaua Ave., Suite 801 **Inside Address**
Honolulu, HI 96815

Dear Sirs: **Salutation**

My class has been studying the 50 states in Social Studies. I really enjoyed learning about Hawaii. I would like to find out even more about your great state.

I would be grateful for any information you could send me on Hawaii. I am especially interested in Hawaii's tourist attractions. I would also like to learn more about Hawaiian history. Maybe someday I will get the chance to visit your state. **Body**

Thank you for your help. I look forward to hearing from you.

Sincerely, **Closing**
Andrew Newton **Signature**
Andrew Newton

Idaho Travel Council
700 West State Street
Boise, ID 83720

Alaska Tourism Marketing Council
Dept. 201, P.O. Box 110801
Juneau, AK 99811-0801

Colorado Tourism Board
1625 Broadway, Suite 1700
Denver, CO 80202

New York Department of Economic Development
1 Commerce Plaza
Albany, NY 12245

Alabama Bureau of Tourism and Travel
401 Adams Avenue, P.O. Box 4309
Montgomery, AL 36103-4309

North Carolina Division of Travel and Tourism
430 North Salisbury Street
Raleigh, NC 27611

California Office of Tourism
L Street Suite 600
Sacramento, CA 95814

©1997 The Education Center, Inc. • *Lifesaver Lessons*™ • Grade 4 • TEC495

How To Extend The Lesson:

• Have each of your students write a business letter to a local politician. In the letter, instruct him to present his view on an issue of importance in the community—such as pollution, crime prevention, or education.

• Challenge your students to draft letters to the editor of your local newspaper. Pair students; then suggest that each pair take a stand on a local, state, or national issue and offer evidence to support this point of view. If desired, mail the letters to your local paper.

• Have each student bring in a business letter from home—with prior parental approval. Label six paper bags, each with the name of a different business-letter part. Instruct each student to cut apart her letter into its six components. Then direct the student to place each of her letter parts in its corresponding bag. Afterward allow each child to select one letter part from each of the six bags. Instruct the student to glue the six letter parts together so that they form an interesting and entirely different business letter. Have volunteers share these new versions with the class.

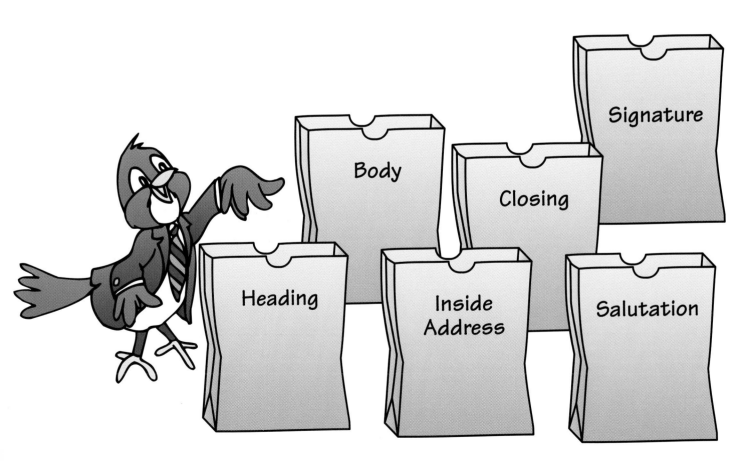

Blueprints For Poetry

Free your students to write poems easily by using planned models.

Skill: Using a model to write a poem

Estimated Lesson Time: 45 minutes

Teacher Preparation:
Duplicate one copy of the reproducible on page 49 for each student.

Materials:
1 sheet of loose-leaf paper for each student
1 pencil for each student
1 copy of page 49 for each student
crayons or colored pencils for each student
scissors, optional (see Step 7 on page 48)

Background Information:
Some students need the support of simple, fill-in-the-blank forms when writing poetry. Using a model allows children to express themselves creatively without being overly concerned about form.

Introducing The Lesson:

Conduct a poll to determine the color most preferred by your students. Then copy the form below onto the chalkboard, writing the winning color at the beginning of each line. Afterward elicit words and phrases from your students to complete each line's thought.

_____	makes me think of _____
_____	looks like _____
_____	tastes like _____
_____	sounds like _____
_____	smells like _____
_____	feels like _____
_____	is the season of _____

Steps:

1. Help your students conclude that they just helped to compose a poem.

2. Have each student copy the form below onto a sheet of loose-leaf paper.

_____	is the color of _____
_____	wishes that _____
_____	remembers _____
_____	is a sign of _____

3. Direct each student to choose an emotion or quality such as *love, hope, peace, war, joy, courage, guilt, strength, anger, happiness,* or *sadness.* Have each student write the word he selected at the beginning of each line on his paper.

4. Allow about ten minutes for your students to complete their poems.

5. Have volunteers share their poems aloud.

6. For more practice, give each student a copy of the reproducible on page 49.

7. If desired, have your students cut out their decorated frames and display them on a bulletin board titled "Reflecting Upon Nature."

Surrounded By Nature

Directions: Follow the steps below to create a poem about nature.

1. Choose something in nature such as the sun, the moon, the sky, a cloud, a river, or a butterfly.
2. Write your topic at the beginning of each line below.
3. Finish the thought in each line of your poem.
4. Copy and illustrate your completed poem inside the picture frame below.
5. Then color the frame.

_____ dreams about _____

_____ remembers _____

_____ is the promise of _____

_____ knows about _____

_____ reminds me of _____

_____ wishes that _____

_____ shows us about _____

Bonus Box: On another sheet of paper and using the model above, write a different poem about a month or season.

©1997 The Education Center, Inc. • *Lifesaver Lessons*™ • Grade 4 • TEC495

How To Extend The Lesson:

- Together, review the haiku form of poetry with your class by writing about an insect. Remind your students that this Japanese form of poetry uses a pattern of syllables to capture a moment in which the natural world is linked to human nature. On the board, write the haiku pattern of syllables as a reference for your students: five syllables in the first line, seven in the second line, and five in the third line. Then challenge each student to write and illustrate a haiku about a different insect for display in the classroom.

- Write the cinquain shown below on the board; then read it aloud. Afterward point out that the poem consists of five lines, with two, four, six, eight, and two syllables respectively. Then have each student write his own cinquain about either a fall, winter, spring, or summer storm. Direct the student to copy his poem onto a sheet of white paper. Next have him mount the white paper onto a larger sheet of colored construction paper. Finally instruct each student to decorate the border of his construction paper with a repeating pattern related to his poem.

- Have each student write an acrostic using the letters of his or her name. Explain that the acrostic should reflect that student's personality and interests. Collect the acrostics and read them aloud one at a time, asking your students to guess the author of each poem.

HAIKU

Busy little ant...
how do you carry a load
heavier than you?

CINQUAIN

Seashells
Wash up on shore
And find a place to rest.
I wonder who will pick them up?
Seashells

A
C
R
O
S
T
I
C
S

Pet Peeves

Unleash your students' pet peeves to create truly unique poems!

Skill: Writing free verse

Estimated Lesson Time: 45 minutes

Teacher Preparation:
Duplicate one copy of page 53 for each student.

Materials:
1 copy of page 53 for each student
chalkboard and chalk
scissors
crayons
pencil and paper

Background Information:
Poems express ideas, emotions, and stories. *Free verse* is poetry written without structure, ending rhyme, or meter. However, this poetic form should have intentional line breaks and contain one or more of the following elements: *metaphor, simile, personification, imagery,* and/or *alliteration.*

- *Metaphor*—the comparison of two unrelated nouns
- *Simile*—a comparison between two unrelated nouns using "like" or "as"
- *Personification*—assigning human traits to things, colors, and ideas
- *Imagery*—creating a mental picture with words
- *Alliteration*—the repetition of the same beginning sound in two or more words that are close together

Introducing The Lesson:

Pose the following questions to your class: "Do you ever get irritated by the annoying habits of others?" and "Are there certain behaviors that *really* bug you?" Explain to students that habits, actions, and behaviors that frustrate us and cause us to complain are called *pet peeves*.

Steps:

1. After introducing and explaining the meaning of pet peeves, list some of your own pet peeves on the board. Describe in detail how each pet peeve makes you feel.

2. Solicit your students' pet peeves and list them on the board. Caution the students to describe their pet peeves without naming any names.

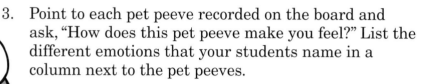

3. Point to each pet peeve recorded on the board and ask, "How does this pet peeve make you feel?" List the different emotions that your students name in a column next to the pet peeves.

4. Write the free-verse poem below on the board; then read the poem aloud to your students. Explain that this poem has no ending rhyme or meter and no particular structure. Point out, though, that this sample poem does have intentional line breaks and contains alliteration (the repeated sound of *p*).

Peter's pet peeve is particularly well known to his brother, Paul. When Paul takes something that Peter owns, Peter *definitely* doesn't consider it a loan...no way!

5. Discuss the other elements that a free-verse poem can contain: *metaphor, simile, personification,* and *imagery* (see page 51).

6. Give each student a copy of page 53. Then have your students take out crayons, scissors, pencils, and paper.

7. Direct each student to follow the directions on his reproducible.

8. Display the resulting pet-peeve characters on a wall or bulletin board in your classroom.

Pet-Peeve Poems

Here's your chance to tell about a pet peeve that *really* bugs you! Follow the directions below to write a nonrhyming poem about one of your pet peeves.

Directions:

1. Choose two of the pet peeves listed on the board.
2. Write a different free-verse poem about each one of these pet peeves on a separate sheet of paper.
3. In each poem, use one or more of the emotions from the list on the board.
4. Also include one of the following elements of poetry in each of your poems: metaphor, simile, personification, imagery, or alliteration.
5. Make each poem 6–8 lines long.
6. Edit your favorite one of the two poems; then copy its final draft on the pet-peeve character below.
7. Color your character, except for the writing lines; then cut out your character for display.

Bonus Box: On another sheet of paper, write a story about a character named Pet Peeve.

by _____

©1997 The Education Center, Inc. • *Lifesaver Lessons*™ • Grade 4 • TEC495

How To Extend The Lesson:

- Explain that the opposite of a pet peeve is something that brings a person quiet pleasure. Brainstorm a list of quiet pleasures with your class. Then have each student write a free-verse poem about one of these joyful moments to share with the class.

- Increase your students' interest in writing free-verse poems by encouraging them to bring in pictures of their pets. If a student does not have a pet, allow him to create an imaginary pet for this one activity. Then instruct each student to write a free-verse poem that describes a humorous episode involving his pet.

- Share one of your favorite free-verse poems—perhaps one written by Walt Whitman. Afterward challenge your students to add another verse to the poem.

- Survey your students to find out whether they agree or disagree that the pet peeves below are commonly shared by lots of different people. Afterward have your students graph the results of this survey.

Pet Peeves

1. The sound of fingers drumming on a desk.
2. The sound of fingernails scraping across a chalkboard.
3. The sound of a dripping faucet.
4. Someone bumping into you or your desk.
5. Someone talking with his mouth full of food.

A Simile Jamboree!

Help your students understand and use similes as they write.

Skill: Using similes to write creatively

Estimated Lesson Time: 45 minutes

Teacher Preparation:
1. Copy the similes from the list below onto a poster.
2. Duplicate one copy of the reproducible on page 57 for each student.

Materials:
1 copy of page 57 for each student
scissors for each student, optional (see step 7 on page 56)
crayons or colored pencils for each student, optional (see step 7 on page 56)

as thin as a rail

Background Information:
A *simile* is a figure of speech that makes a comparison between two different nouns using *like* or *as*. Some common similes are:

as light as a feather	as quiet as a mouse
as cold as ice	as stubborn as a mule
as green as grass	as dry as a bone
as smooth as glass	as soft as silk
as hard as a rock	as thin as a rail
as strong as an ox	as deep as the ocean
as cute as a button	as clear as day
as dark as night	as white as snow
as busy as a bee	laughed like a hyena
as hungry as a bear	like a fish out of water
as sly as a fox	waddled like a duck
as sweet as honey	worked like a horse
as quick as a wink	sparkled like diamonds

Introducing The Lesson:

Write the following sentence on the chalkboard: "My cat is as silent as a sunset." Have your students listen as you read the sentence aloud; then ask them to identify the two things that are being compared in the sentence *(the cat* and *the sunset).*

Steps:

1. Review the definition of a simile (see page 55); then display the poster of similes that you made earlier.

2. Select a student to read aloud the similes that use *as.* Afterward choose a different student to read aloud the similes that feature *like.*

3. Write the word *broom* on the board. Ask your students to think of an adjective that describes this noun, such as *gigantic* broom. Next have the class think of another noun that can be described by this adjective. For instance, a *skyscraper* can also be gigantic. Then piece together the words to form a comparative sentence: *A skyscraper is like a gigantic broom that sweeps the sky.*

4. Pair your students; then have each pair of students choose a different noun. Direct each pair to follow the process in step 3 to create a comparative sentence to share with the class.

5. As each pair shares its comparative sentence, record it on the board and point out the two nouns being compared.

6. For additional practice, give each student a copy of the reproducible on page 57.

7. If desired, have each student color and cut out his pie shape from the reproducible. Then display all the pie shapes on a bulletin board titled "Similes Are As Easy As Pie!"

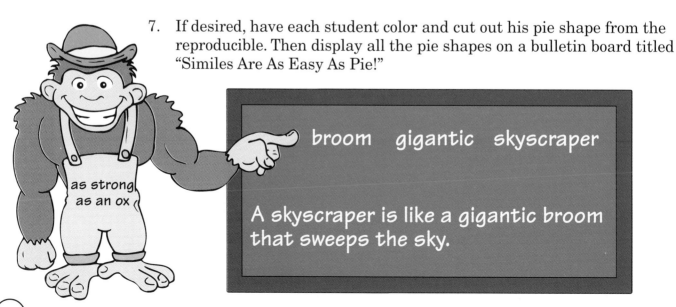

As Easy As Pie!

Directions: Follow the steps below to create a simile about a pie.

1. Write the name of a pie on the first blank line in Part A and in Part B below. For example, *ice-cream pie* and *strawberry pie.*

2. On the next blank line in each part, compare each pie to another noun. Then on the last blank line, explain why the pie is like that noun. For example: *Ice-cream pie* is like *pudding* because *it's creamy. Strawberry pie* is like *a rose* because *it is red.*

3. Next piece the important words together to form a comparative sentence and write it on the line provided. For example: *Ice-cream pie is as creamy as pudding. Strawberry pie is as red as a rose.*

4. Choose one of your comparative sentences to use as the first line of a poem about your pie. Think of additional comparative sentences to add to your poem; then write your poem on the lines of the pie at the bottom of this sheet.

5. Color the outer edges of the pie to make it resemble the pie in your poem.

> as cute
> as a
> button

Part A:

_____ is like _____

because _____.

Sentence: _____

Part B:

_____ is like _____

because _____.

Sentence: _____

How To Extend The Lesson:

- Play a competitive game to give your students more practice with similes. Divide your students into teams of four. Appoint one student on each team to be the recorder. Explain that you will write an incomplete simile on the board and the members of each team should work together to fill in the blanks of this simile with appropriate nouns. Establish that each recorder should copy the simile from the board, write the nouns suggested by his group's members, and raise his hand when he's finished writing. Then, on the board, write "_____ is as fast as _____ on a windy day." Signal the groups to begin working; then call, "Stop," when you see a reporter raising his hand. If that reporter answers with appropriate nouns, give that group one point. For example, "A *four-wheeler* is as fast as *a cloud* on a windy day." Play additional rounds by substituting *fast* in the given example with *kind, happy, round, square, big, wide, flat, crooked, high, red, stubborn, brave, thick, caring, mad, blue, dark, white,* or *wise.* In addition, provide an appropriate ending phrase for the simile in each round.

- Have each student choose a word that names a color and write that word on a sheet of white drawing paper. Then direct the student to tell what that color looks like, smells like, tastes like, feels like, and sounds like. For example, to explain what green smells like, a student could write "Green smells like the air when the grass has just been cut." Finally, have the student illustrate the descriptions on her paper.

- Assign each student a different letter of the alphabet. Challenge the student to write a poem about his assigned letter that includes at least one simile. Then have each student copy his poem onto a large cutout of his letter's shape. Display the letters in an alphabetical arrangement on a bulletin board or wall space titled "ABC Similes."

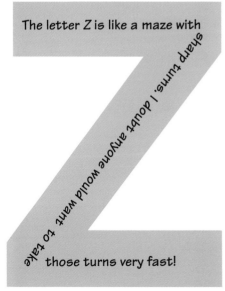

The letter Z is like a maze with sharp turns. I doubt anyone would want to take those turns very fast!

Sounds Simply Sensational!

Help your students understand and use alliteration as they write.

Skill: Using alliteration to write creatively

Estimated Lesson Time: 45 minutes

Teacher Preparation:
Duplicate a copy of page 61 for each student.

Materials:
1 copy of page 61 for each student
1/4 sheet of poster board for each student
colored markers, crayons, or colored pencils
dictionaries: one for each student

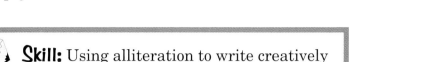

Background Information:
Alliteration is the repetition of the same consonant sound at the beginnings of words. For example, **B**enny's **B**ig **B**and **b**ellowed at **L**ucky **L**ou's in **L**ouisville.

Introducing The Lesson:

Hold a picture of a kitten in your hand. Ask your students to help you describe the kitten using words with the same beginning sounds. Expect responses such as *kitty cat, cute kitten, cuddly kitten, curious kitten*, etc.

Steps:

1. Explain that writers repeat the same beginning sounds of words to create vivid images for their readers. Provide several examples of alliteration that clarify this statement—such as *the silky, soft snow; a blasting bullet; the whispering wind; a glittering, green glaze; the moldable mud;* and *a tasty tomato.*

2. Write the sentence fragments below on the board. Have your students complete the fragments using alliteration. Then discuss the impact of alliteration on each completed sentence.

   Bertha Baccio bought…
   Friendly Frederick found…
   Stephen steadily…
   George just…
   Mary might mean…

3. Assign one letter of the alphabet to each student. Direct the student to list interesting words and names that begin with the same sound as his letter. Suggest that he use a dictionary to help him extend his list.

4. Have each student construct a sentence that uses as many of the words in his list as possible.

5. Give each student a small piece of poster board. In one corner of this poster board, have him write his assigned letter in a bold and fancy manner. Across the bottom of his poster board, instruct him to write his sentence. Then direct him to illustrate his sentence in the remaining space on the poster board.

6. Display your students' work along a wall in alphabetical order. Or bind the pieces together as an alliterative alphabet book to donate to a kindergarten or first-grade class.

7. Then give each student a copy of page 61 to complete for independent practice.

Sounds Simply Sensational!

Part One: Jazz up the following sentences with words that have the same beginning sounds. Then complete the activities in Part Two.

1. _____ Patricia purchased _____ _____ for _____.

2. Joyce just _____ a jet for _____ so that she could _____ her _____.

3. Did _____ Dan _____ the _____ to _____?

4. Matthew made _____ on _____.

5. _____ Clancy can't _____ 'cause his _____ _____.

Part Two: Think of a letter other than *p, j, d, m,* or *c.* Write this letter in the blank below. Then use a dictionary to help you find nouns, verbs, and adjectives that begin with this new letter. Write the words that you find in the categories below.

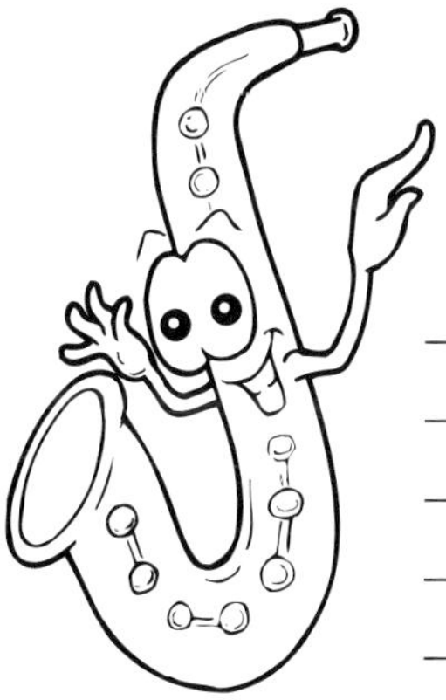

_____
letter

Nouns	**Verbs**	**Adjectives**
_____	_____	_____
_____	_____	_____
_____	_____	_____
_____	_____	_____

Now, on the lines below, write several silly sentences using as many of these words as you can!

1. _____

2. _____

3. _____

4. _____

5. _____

Bonus Box: On the back of this sheet, use some words from the categories above to write an alliterative poem that sounds simply sensational!

61

How To Extend The Lesson:

- Review alliteration by playing a fun variation of Grandmother's Trunk. Have your students sit in a circle. Start the game by asking one student to choose a letter of the alphabet. Have this student make up a name and a place that begin with that letter. Then direct her to say, "[Made-up name] is going to [made-up place] and in his/her trunk s/he packed…" Then, in turn, have each student think of an additional item to pack that begins with the same sound. Direct the last student to take a turn to start the next round.

- Challenge your students to find examples of alliteration in unusual places. Suggest that your young detectives search through atlases and maps to find alliterative place names—such as Vernon, Vermont, or Saskatoon, Saskatchewan. Or have your supersleuths use encyclopedias or phone books to find alliterative names like Howard Hughes or Richard Rogers. Compile your students' findings in a class book.

- Allow each student to transform one of his silly sentences from the reproducible on page 61 into a silly story. Give each student one sheet of duplicating paper. Instruct him to fold this paper in half from top to bottom. Next have him cut his paper along its fold line to create two matching halves. Then direct him to stack these two matching halves atop one another and fold them in half from left to right. Instruct him to staple these pages along their folded edges to create a minibook with four pages. Afterward have the student use these pages—front and back—for writing and illustrating a story about one of his silly sentences.

- Tangle your students' tongues with good, old-fashioned tongue twisters. Remind them about *Peter Piper picked a peck of pickled peppers* and *She sells seashells by the seashore*. Then challenge your students to create tongue twisters of their own. Afterward allow your students to exchange their tongue-twisting creations with one another for a hilariously good time!

Peter Piper picked a peck of pickled peppers.

Follow The Signs To Sequencing

Keep your students focused on a path to better comprehension with this sequencing lesson.

Skills: Putting events in sequential order; recognizing and using words that indicate sequence

Estimated Lesson Time: 45 minutes

Teacher Preparation:
1. Duplicate one copy of page 65 for each student.
2. Select a favorite short story with events occurring in sequential order.

Materials:
1 sheet of chart paper
1 copy of page 65 for each student
1 preselected short story

Background Information:
Many words signal the time order in which a series of events occur. Some of these time-signal words are listed below.

first	during
second	when
third	finally
meanwhile	later
then	while
next	before
after	last

Introducing The Lesson:

Explain to your students that an author tells the events of his story in a certain order or sequence with the help of specific signal words. Then read aloud a short story of your choice. Afterward ask your students to retell the events of this story in sequential order—as they remember them. Record these events on the board as your students dictate them.

Steps:

1. Ask your students to recall specific words from the story that helped them sequence its events. List these words on the board.

2. Next have your students brainstorm other words used by authors to indicate sequence (see page 63). Record both the words suggested by your students and those from page 63 on a sheet of chart paper. Post this chart in your room as a reference for your students.

3. Explain how signal words aid in understanding a story by pointing out the order in which its events occur.

4. Discuss why it is important to understand the order of events when reading or listening to a story. Point out how a story's meaning might change if the order of its events were altered or misunderstood. Illustrate this point by asking students what would happen if the steps of a recipe were switched. Have volunteers make predictions about how or if such a change in steps could affect a recipe's outcome.

Spread the jelly on the bread.

Spread the peanut butter on the bread.

5. Provide each student with a copy of page 65. Then instruct your students to complete the sheet according to its directions. Remind your students to look for signal words as sequence clues.

6. Check page 65 together as a class to review sequence words. Discuss the role played by each signal word in understanding the correct order of the sheet's events.

Follow The Signs To Sequencing

Directions: Read each group of sentences in each section below. Show the order of each section's events by writing a *1, 2,* or *3* in the blank before each sentence. Then follow the directions at the bottom of this page to decode a secret message.

FIRST

MEANWHILE

A. _____ Jennifer washed her hands with <u>the</u> new soap.
_____ Finally, Jennifer sat down <u>to</u> eat dinner with her family.
_____ Then she dried her <u>hands</u>.

B. _____ First I asked <u>for</u> a hamburger and fries.
_____ Then I changed my order <u>to</u> chicken fingers.
_____ After I arrived at the restaurant, I looked at the menu to help me decide what to <u>order</u>.

NEXT

C. _____ Jan bought a bag <u>of</u> candy.
_____ Then she removed several pieces of candy and resealed <u>the</u> bag.
_____ She opened the <u>bag</u> carefully.

THIRD

D. _____ We have several <u>events</u> planned for the picnic.
_____ Then we <u>are</u> going to have a relay race.
_____ First we are going to <u>have</u> a pie-eating contest.

THEN

E. _____ Finally, he <u>will</u> put his clothes in the soapy water.
_____ Next he will add <u>some</u> detergent.
_____ James <u>is</u> going to turn on the water to wash his dirty clothes.

AFTER

F. _____ We <u>celebrate</u> it by having cake and ice cream.
_____ Jake's birthday is an <u>important</u> day for our family.
_____ Afterwards we play <u>games</u>.

BEFORE

Now look back at the sentence in each section that you marked with a "1." Write the underlined words from those sentences in A–F order in the blanks below. If you marked your sentences correctly and recorded the underlined words in the right order, they will reveal a special message.

_____   _____   _____
             A   B   C

_____   _____   _____
             D   E   F

Bonus Box: On the back of this sheet, write the steps that tell how you get ready for school in an out-of-order sequence. Then have a classmate number your steps to show them in their correct order.

©1997 The Education Center, Inc. • *Lifesaver Lessons*™ • Grade 4 • TEC495 • Key p. 95

How To Extend The Lesson:

- Record several sentences from your current read-aloud on sentence strips. Then cut each sentence apart into its separate words. Place each set of words that makes a sentence inside a different envelope. Next divide your class into groups of three to four students each. Distribute a different envelope to each group. Allow each group two minutes to arrange its words in an order that makes a sentence. Have the group then replace that sentence's words in its envelope and pass it to the next group. After all of the envelopes have circulated through each group, review the correct answers one envelope at a time with your class. Discuss the importance of placing words within a sentence in the correct sequence.

- Remove several short stories from old books or magazines. Next cut the stories apart by paragraphs. Then place the paragraphs for each story inside different 8 1/2" x 11" brown envelopes. Have your students follow the same procedure described in the first extension on this page to arrange the paragraphs for each story in the correct order.

- Have each student bring in one comic strip from the newspaper. Ask the student to cut apart his comic strip, shuffle its frames, and hold the frames together with a paper clip. Collect all of the clipped comic strips; then distribute the comic strips so that no student has his own strip. Direct each student to arrange the frames in his set in their correct sequence. Afterward have him write a creative narrative to accompany his comic strip. Instruct the student to glue the frames of his comic strip to the bottom of his narrative in the correct order. Display the final versions of your students' narratives and comics in your room for everyone to enjoy.

- Pair your students and assign each pair a different short story. Next have each pair read its short story and record all of the sequencing words found in it. Then have each pair share its findings with the rest of the class. During each pair's presentation, if any sequencing words were discovered by the pair in its search that were different from the ones already listed, add them to the class chart.

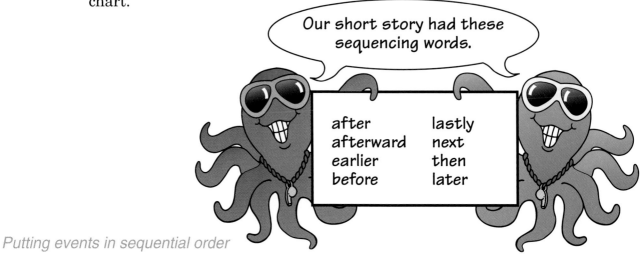

Pointed In The Right Direction!

Sharpen your students' comprehension skills with story maps.

Skill: Recognizing and describing the elements of a story

Estimated Lesson Time: 45 minutes

Teacher Preparation:
1. Gather a map of your city or county.
2. Duplicate a copy of page 69 for each student.
3. Select a familiar fairy tale to share with students.

Materials:
manila paper, 4 sheets (18" x 24") for each student

letter-size envelopes, 7 for each student

3" x 5" index cards, 7 for each student

crayons, markers, and pencils

a stapler

glue

a copy of page 69 for each student

Background Information:
A *story map* is a method of graphically organizing the elements of a story. It is constructed by listing the elements as headings in an arrangement that resembles a simple map. This maplike arrangement helps a student understand the relationship among a story's elements. The elements of a story are:

- *Setting*—the place and time during which a story's action occurs
- *Characters*—the people or animals in a story
- *Plot*—the problem that needs to be solved, including the sequential events that lead to its solution
- *Climax*—the event that brings about a solution to the story's problem
- *Ending*—the conclusion of the story
- *Theme*—the main idea of the story

Mapping a story 67

Introducing The Lesson:

Display a city or county map and have student volunteers find the street location of your school and other places of interest. Help students conclude that maps allow its users to see the relationship of streets and other physical locations.

Steps:

1. Explain to students that stories—like cities—can be mapped so that readers can understand the relationship of a story's elements.

2. List the following story elements across the chalkboard in six columns: setting, characters, plot, climax, ending, and theme.

3. Retell a brief version of the fairy tale that you selected.

4. Explain the story elements listed on the board one at a time (see page 67). After each explanation, ask your students to name that particular element from the fairy tale that you shared. List each response on the board under its appropriate heading.

5. Give each student a copy of the reproducible on page 69. Have the student complete the sheet using information from a book he recently read.

6. Place the resulting booklets in a reading center for your students to enjoy during their free time.

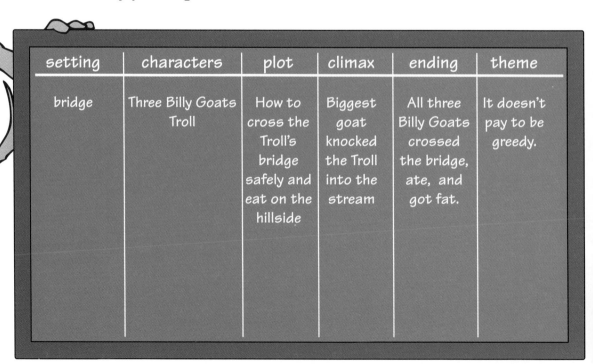

setting	characters	plot	climax	ending	theme
bridge	Three Billy Goats Troll	How to cross the Troll's bridge safely and eat on the hillside	Biggest goat knocked the Troll into the stream	All three Billy Goats crossed the bridge, ate, and got fat.	It doesn't pay to be greedy.

Point Me In The Right Direction!

Follow the directions below to create a question-and-answer booklet that maps the elements of a story you recently read.

What You Need:
4 sheets of 18" x 24" manila paper
7 small envelopes
7 index cards, 3" x 5"
crayons or markers
a pencil
a stapler
glue

Directions:

1. Stack your four sheets of manila paper on top of one another; then fold these sheets in half and staple them along the fold at the top to create a booklet with eight pages.

2. Decorate the cover of this booklet. Be sure to include your book's title and author on the cover.

3. Glue an envelope—flap side out—to the lower right half of each right-hand page.

4. Write a question about the main characters of your story in your booklet. For example, on a page above one of the envelopes, write "Who are the main characters in this story? Describe them." Write the answer to this question on an index card; then place this card inside the envelope on that page. Do **not** seal the envelope.

5. In this same manner, write a question on a page and an answer on an index card for each of the remaining story elements—the setting, plot, climax, ending, and theme. Be sure that each index card is placed in the appropriate envelope.

6. Draw a picture on the left-hand half of each page that illustrates the question on the right-hand half of the page.

7. Write your name, your rating of this book, and your reasons for this rating on the last page of your booklet.

8. Ask yourself what you would change about the story. Write your suggestions on the one remaining index card; then place this card inside the envelope on the last page. Be sure to illustrate this answer as well.

©1997 The Education Center, Inc. • *Lifesaver Lessons*™ • Grade 4 • TEC495

How To Extend The Lesson:

• Tell your students a familiar story, one element at a time. Begin with this story's theme and work backward to its most familiar element—the plot. Set a timer to see how long it takes your students to recognize this story. Allow volunteers to share other well-known stories in this manner as well.

• Poll your students to see how many of them have read a particular story. Challenge these students to work together as a group. Have each group member choose a different element of that story to share with the class. Further challenge each member by having him assume the persona of one of that story's main characters as he shares his particular story element!

• Divide your students into six groups; then give each group a sheet of poster board. Assign each group a different story element from the list on page 67. Have each group design a poster that includes a definition, an example, and an illustration of its assigned element. Display these posters as reminders of the six story elements.

Characters—the people or animals in a story

Example: Sarge, a bird dog

The Tie That Binds!

Unwrap the wealth of information available in the dictionary with this word-relation activity.

Skills: Alphabetizing words; reading phonetic spellings; comparing word meanings

Estimated Lesson Time: 45 minutes

Teacher Preparation:
1. Duplicate one copy of page 73 for each student.
2. Gather one dictionary for every two students in your class.

Materials:
1 copy of page 73 for each student
1 dictionary for each pair of students

Background Information:
A dictionary is a resource that includes an alphabetical listing and other information about the words it contains. Dictionaries give the correct spelling, capitalization, syllabication, accent marks, pronunciation, part of speech, word history, synonyms and antonyms, and meaning for each entry.

Introducing The Lesson:

Write *foxglove, clematis,* and *anemone* on the board. Have your students explain how these three words are alike. Allow your students time to reflect; then ask them if they know of a resource that could make their task easier. Help your students conclude that a dictionary would be a helpful tool for identifying words that are similar.

Steps:

1. Select three students; then assign each student one of the words written on the board. Have each student look up the meaning of his word and share its meaning aloud with the class. Challenge the other students to listen carefully to each definition and determine how the three words are related. Guide your students to conclude that the three words are names of different types of flowers.

2. Pair your students; then give each pair a dictionary.

3. Have your students brainstorm the ways that a dictionary is helpful. Record your students' suggestions on the board.

4. Review the different types of information available in a dictionary. To do this, randomly select several entry words; then have your students point out the different components of each entry (see page 71).

5. Give each student a copy of page 73. Direct each pair to share a dictionary to complete their worksheets.

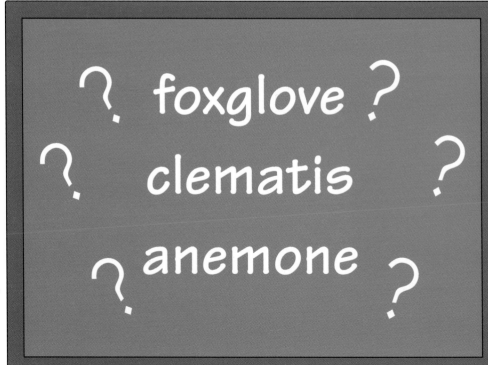

The Tie That Binds

Directions: Look at the three words on each package below. Find the definition of each word in the dictionary. Compare the definitions of each set of words to discover how they are alike. On the bow of each package, write a classification for that set of words. For example, *boots, high heels,* and *sneakers* would be classified as *shoes.* Then alphabetize each set of words by writing a *1, 2,* or *3* in the blank next to each word to show the order that it would appear in the dictionary.

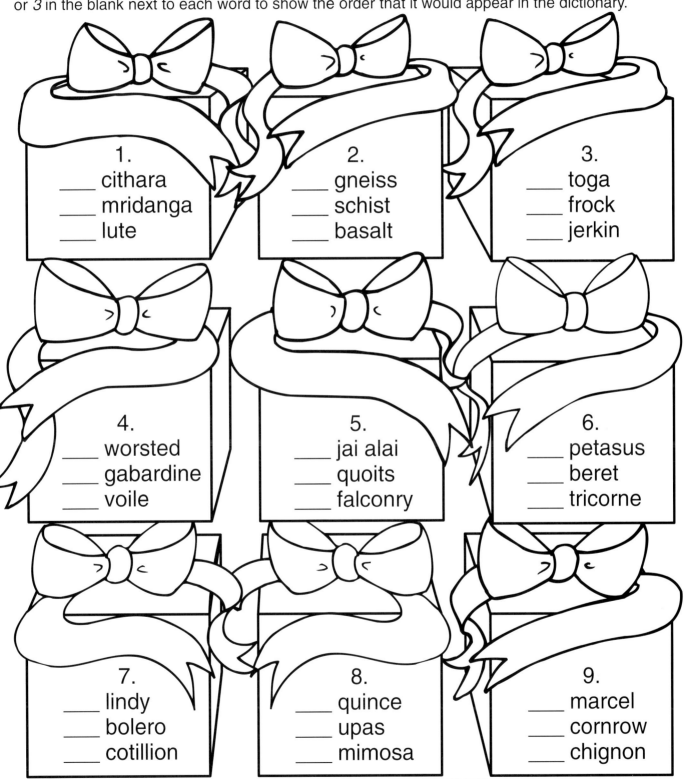

1.
___ cithara
___ mridanga
___ lute

2.
___ gneiss
___ schist
___ basalt

3.
___ toga
___ frock
___ jerkin

4.
___ worsted
___ gabardine
___ voile

5.
___ jai alai
___ quoits
___ falconry

6.
___ petasus
___ beret
___ tricorne

7.
___ lindy
___ bolero
___ cotillion

8.
___ quince
___ upas
___ mimosa

9.
___ marcel
___ cornrow
___ chignon

Bonus Box: On the back of this sheet, draw another gift box similar to those above. On this box, write three words that are related in some way.

How To Extend The Lesson:

- Divide your class into four groups for a dictionary scavenger hunt. Give each group several dictionaries; then have group members work together to find the answer to one question at a time from the list below. Instruct each group to signal when it finds an answer by having all its members raise their hands.
  1. Who would use a *balk line?* *(someone shooting pool)*
  2. What nation refers to its money as *krona? (Sweden and Iceland)*
  3. From what country do *Lhasa apso* dogs originate? *(Tibet)*
  4. How many entries are given in the dictionary for the word *scribe?* *(varies depending on the dictionary consulted)*
  5. Which syllable is accented in the word *bibliography? (third)*
  6. What are the guide words for the entry word *potato? (answers will vary depending on which dictionary is consulted)*
  7. What are the guide words for the entry word *insect? (answers will vary depending on dictionary consulted)*
  8. Would it be polite to refer to someone as a *dolt? (no)*
  9. Is a book *esculent? (no)*
  10. On what continent do *warthogs* reside? *(Africa)*

- Turn a file box into a class dictionary. Purchase a file box along with some index cards and alphabetical dividers. Every time a student encounters unfamiliar words, have him write each word at the top of a different index card, followed by its definition. Next have the student use that word in a sentence or provide an illustration of it on the back of the card. Have him file each card alphabetically in the file box. Then periodically use this file box as a resource for a challenging vocabulary game for your students.

- Write a word on the board that is unfamiliar to your students. Use this word in a sentence. Then have each student write a definition for this word on a scrap sheet of paper, reminding him that what he writes will be a guess. Collect your students' papers. Read the actual definition for this word along with several of your students' definitions—without revealing that the real definition is mixed in with the others. Have your students guess which definition is the correct one. Afterward discuss how context clues can be used to determine the meaning of a new word. Repeat this procedure with several other new words.

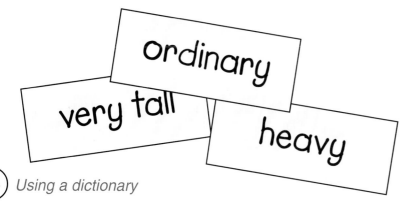

Extra! Extra! Read All About It!

Get the scoop on unknown words by using context clues.

Skill: Using context clues to determine the meanings of unknown words

Estimated Time Needed: 45 minutes

Teacher Preparation:
1. Duplicate one copy of page 77 for each student.
2. Clip five short newspaper articles from your local paper. Then make enough copies of these articles so that each student will receive one article.

Materials:
1 copy of page 69 for each student
1 copy of a newspaper article for each student

Background Information:
Context clues are all the other words that help unlock the meanings of unfamiliar words. A context clue can be positioned before or after an unknown word, within the same sentence, or in another sentence. Context clues may compare words, describe words, or restate an idea.

Introducing The Lesson:

Begin this lesson by writing the following sentences on the board: *The excitement of the field trip has Mrs. Kane's students in a <u>jovial</u> mood. She has never seen them so happy!* Ask each student to think about the meaning of the underlined word in the first sentence; then call on several students and have them explain how they determined the meaning of this word.

Steps:

1. Explain what context clues are, where they can be found, and how they can be used (see page 75).

2. Distribute one copy of page 77 to each student. Give your students 10–15 minutes to complete this sheet.

3. Check the answers to this sheet together. Afterward randomly distribute one copy of one of the newspaper articles duplicated earlier to each student.

4. Instruct each student to read her article and underline three words that are unfamiliar to her. Next have her determine the meanings of these unknown words by using context clues.

5. Then give her an index card on which to write one of her words and its definition.

6. Post your students' index cards on a bulletin board that has been covered with sheets of newspaper and titled "Newsworthy Words."

> The excitement of the field trip has Mrs. Kane's students in a <u>jovial</u> mood. She has never seen them so happy!

Extra! Extra! Read All About It!

Here's the scoop! Each paragraph below tells something about newspapers and how they are made. Read each paragraph to find the meaning of its headline. Next write the meaning of that headline on the lines below each paragraph. Then underline the clues in each paragraph that helped you understand each headline's meaning.

1.

Newsprint

A newspaper tells about and comments on the news. Sixty million copies of daily newspapers are circulated throughout the United States every day. Newspapers are printed on newsprint, a coarse paper made from wood pulp.

_____

_____

_____

_____

2.

Tabloid

The two most common sizes of newspapers are standard and tabloid. A standard-sized newspaper measures about 13 x 21 1/2 inches. A tabloid's pages are about half the size of a standard newspaper's pages. Tabloids report the news with lots of pictures, larger headlines, and shorter articles.

_____

_____

_____

_____

3.

Beat Reporters

Newspapers use different kinds of reporters. General reporters cover any story to which they are assigned. Reporters who cover news in one particular location or about one particular subject are called beat reporters. For example, a beat reporter may report only the news from city hall or about education.

_____

_____

_____

_____

4.

Lead

Reporters start each news story with a lead—the first paragraph, which contains important facts. The reporter then completes the story with details that tell who, what, when, where, why, and/or how.

_____

_____

_____

_____

5.

Copy Editor

A reporter's completed story is taken to someone who checks it for accuracy and writes a headline for it. This person may change some words to make the article easier to understand or cut some information if the story is too long. The person responsible for this job is called a copy editor.

_____

_____

_____

_____

6.

Layout

Artists create a layout—or sketch—of each newspaper page. Most newspaper artists are able to quickly plan where each story, picture, and advertisement will be placed on a page by using computers.

_____

_____

_____

_____

Bonus Box: Look back at each news article above. On the back of this page, tell whether the context clues for each article come before the unfamiliar word, after the unknown word, or in another sentence.

77

How To Extend The Lesson:

• Follow the model below to create a learning-center activity that reinforces the use of context clues. Program several index cards with sentences that contain missing words. Write a different sentence on the front of each card and its self-checking answer on the back. Direct each student to use the context of each sentence to determine its missing word (see the example).

> Timothy quickly made a wish and then blew out the ten candles atop his _____ cake. *(birthday)*

• Create some made-up words such as *miojk, tunghy,* and *reirsg.* Assign each student one of these nonsense words; then challenge him to make up a sentence or paragraph that supplies clues to the meaning of his assigned word. Afterward have the student share his writing and allow his classmates to guess his intended meaning for the word.

• Challenge your students to use context clues to determine the meanings of assigned vocabulary words from your current novel. First have each student write what she thinks each vocabulary word means based on its context clues. Then have her compare her meaning with the dictionary's definition to see if she is correct.

Just The Facts—And Opinions, Please!

Investigate the difference between facts and opinions.

 Skills: Distinguishing facts from opinions; recognizing clue words that signal facts and opinions

 Estimated Lesson Time: 45 minutes

Teacher Preparation:
1. Duplicate one copy of page 81 for each student.
2. Gather 20 sentence strips on which to write sentences—ten that give a fact about a topic you are currently studying and ten that give an opinion.

Materials:
20 sentence strips—ten with factual sentences and ten with sentences that give opinions
1 copy of page 81 for each student
green crayons
masking tape

Background Information:
A *fact* is a statement that is true and can be proven. Facts often contain numbers, ages, or dates.

An *opinion* is a statement that reveals what someone believes to be true. Opinions cannot be classified as true or false because they cannot be proven or tested. Some words that signal opinions are *believe, feel, seem, perhaps, all, best, every, never, worst,* and *think.*

Introducing The Lesson:

Ask your students to share what they consider to be the most delicious snack they have ever eaten. Afterward point out the variations in your students' answers. Have your students explain how it is possible to get such different responses to the same question. Help your students conclude that their responses were *opinions*—or statements of personal feeling. Point out that their statements were not facts because they cannot be proven. Next ask your students what the cafeteria served for lunch yesterday. Have your students explain why their responses to this question were the same. Point out that what was served for lunch yesterday can be proven and is, therefore, a *fact*—unlike the answer to the previous question.

Steps:

1. Define *fact* and *opinion* for your students (see page 79).

2. Display the sentence strips—prepared by you in advance—that list various facts and opinions. Ask your class to determine whether the statement featured on each strip is a fact or an opinion. Challenge your students to give the reasons for their decisions.

3. Make two columns—one labeled "Fact" and another labeled "Opinion"—on your chalkboard. Post the fact and opinion strips that you made on the board under their appropriate columns.

4. Have each student write one fact and one opinion on paper. Instruct your students to share their statements aloud one at a time, but without revealing which type of statement they are. After each statement is read, choose another student to classify it as a fact or an opinion. Continue in this manner until every student has shared at least one statement.

5. Give each student a copy of page 81. Instruct your students to complete this sheet according to its directions.

6. Collect the sheets and use them to assess your students' mastery of this skill.

Words That Signal Opinions

believe	best
feel	every
seem	never
perhaps	worst
all	think

Just The Facts, Please!

Directions: Read each statement below and decide whether it is a fact or an opinion. If the statement is a fact, color the eucalyptus leaf next to it green.

FACT: *a statement that is true and can be proven*
OPINION: *a statement of a personal belief or feeling that cannot be proven*

 N 1. Koalas are the cutest animals of all.

 I 2. The koala is a marsupial—or pouched—animal.

S 3. Koalas make their homes in trees.

 M 4. Koalas seem to be happy animals.

 A 5. Eucalyptus leaves do not have a good taste.

 A 6. The average koala bear needs more than a pound of eucalyptus leaves every day.

 E 7. Koala babies are funny-looking animals.

L 8. The word *koala* comes from the word *kaloine* which means "do not drink."

 O 9. Koalas are always very friendly.

U 10. The koala gets its water from the eucalyptus leaves that it eats.

A 11. Koalas sleep 18 to 20 hours a day.

R 12. The female koala raises her young alone.

T 13. Once a baby koala becomes too heavy for its mother's pouch, she shifts the baby to her back.

 C 14. Everyone who has a chance to see a koala will like this animal.

P 15. Koalas should be used as the next Olympic mascot.

A 16. Eucalyptus trees grow in Australia.

Unscramble the letters on the eucalyptus leaves that you colored to find out where koalas live. Spell this location in the blanks below.

___ ___ ___ ___ ___ ___ ___ ___ ___

Bonus Box: Use the back of this sheet to write a poem about a koala that includes two facts and two opinions.

How To Extend The Lesson:

- Have your students read over your local newspaper to search for facts and opinions. Then give each student or group two markers of different colors. Direct your students to use a designated color to highlight all facts and the other color to highlight opinions. For example, have them use yellow for opinions and green for facts. Afterward discuss which sections of the paper seemed to have more opinions and which ones contained more facts. Also discuss the purpose of each of these sections. For example, point out that the front page of the paper is more factual than the editorial page because its purpose is to report facts rather than opinions or different points of view.

- For one day, instruct each student to keep a written log of the facts and opinions that she overhears in conversations. The next day, give each student an opportunity to share her findings with the class. Discuss the different situations in which people were more likely to use factual statements than opinions, cautioning students not to discuss opinions about *people.*

- Challenge your students to write several facts and opinions, each one on a separate strip of paper. Then instruct each student to fold his strips and place them inside a large paper bag labeled "Fact-And-Opinion Sack." After your students have contributed to this sack, shake it. Choose one student to select a strip from the bag. Then have this student read the strip aloud and classify it as a fact or an opinion. Make sure that he also explains the reasons for his choice. For example, *Labor Day is a holiday* would be classified as a fact because it can be proven, while *I like Easter* would be classified as an opinion because it tells how someone feels.

Developing A Case For Cause And Effect

Present this opened-and-closed case for cause and effect!

Skill: Determining the effect of a specific action or cause

Estimated Lesson Time: 45 minutes

Teacher Preparation:
1. Make one copy of page 85 for each of your students.
2. Gather pictures of specific events from old magazines or newspapers.

Materials:
1 ruler
1 penny
1 copy of page 85 for each student
old magazines or newspapers, one for each student
glue
scissors

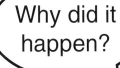

Cause

Effect

Background Information:
An *effect* can be defined as *what happened*. A *cause* can be defined as *why it happened*. An effect can be traced back to a specific cause.

Clue words—such as *when, due to, therefore, as a result of, hence, because,* and *then*—help identify cause and effect relationships.

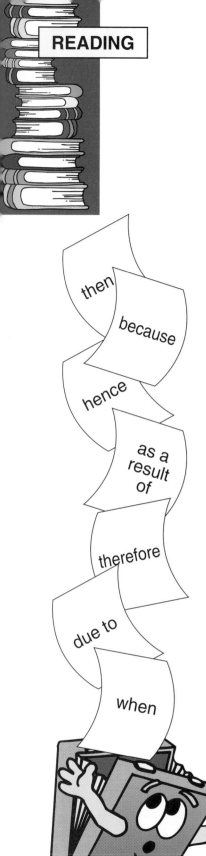

Introducing The Lesson:

Begin this lesson by conducting a simple demonstration of cause and effect for your students. Balance a ruler on the edge of a desk. Ask your students to predict what will happen if you place a penny on the edge of the ruler that hangs off the desk. After your students make their predictions, complete the demonstration. (*The ruler will fall off of the desk due to the increased weight of the penny on one side*.) Discuss the ruler's fall as an effect—or what happened—and the penny's placement on the ruler's edge as the cause—or why it happened.

Steps:

1. Display several pictures that depict specific happenings or effects—such as a parade, an athlete celebrating a victory, a riot, or a citizen receiving an award. Ask your students in turn to offer reasons why the event in each picture happened.

2. Distribute a copy of page 85 to each student. Also give each student an old magazine or newspaper, scissors, and glue.

3. Have each student look through her magazine or newspaper to find four small, interesting pictures.

4. Instruct the student to cut out her four pictures and glue each one to a different suitcase on page 85. Afterward have her write a descriptive caption for each picture on the line labeled "Effect."

5. Then direct each student to list possible causes for each event on the blank lines below each suitcase. For example, if a student selects a picture of a crying baby, suggest that she write "The baby is hungry" and "The baby is tired" as possible causes.

6. After your students have listed the causes and effects for their pictures, ask several volunteers to share their examples with the class.

7. As each volunteer shares, allow your class to suggest other causes that could result in the same effect.

A Case For Cause And Effect

Directions: Follow your teacher's instructions about what to do with the four briefcases below. Then listen carefully to her directions about what to write on each briefcase and the lines below it.

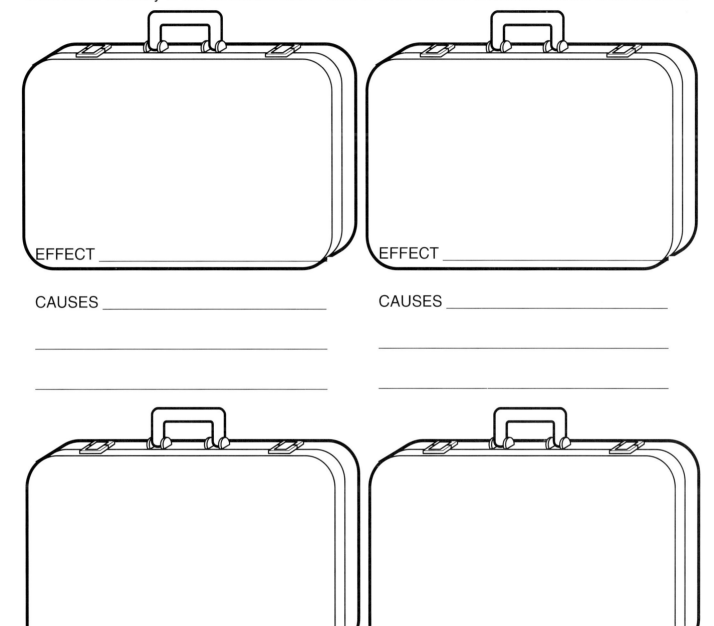

EFFECT _____

CAUSES _____

_____

_____

EFFECT _____

CAUSES _____

_____

_____

EFFECT _____

CAUSES _____

_____

_____

EFFECT _____

CAUSES _____

_____

_____

Bonus Box: On the back of this sheet, list five actions that you have taken today. Then, next to each action, list the cause for each one.

©1997 The Education Center, Inc. • *Lifesaver Lessons*™ • Grade 4 • TEC495

85

How To Extend The Lesson:

- Have each student look through an old newspaper and cut out its weather forecast. Instruct the student to glue this forecast to a sheet of paper and label it "Cause." Then direct the student to explain in writing how this forecast will affect the way she dresses and any plans she makes for recreation and travel. Have her label her reactions to the forecast "Effects."

- Direct your students to generate a list of occupations. Record their responses on the board. Then challenge your students to think of several effects that each occupation has on their lives. For example, help your students conclude that a doctor helps them maintain their health, assists them when they are sick, and researches cures for diseases.

- Write several causes on strips of paper; then place these strips inside a paper bag. Choose a student to draw one strip from the bag and read it aloud to the class. Challenge the other students to generate a list of possible effects for this cause. After suggesting effects for all of your causes, repeat the activity—this time giving your students the opportunity to suggest the causes. Challenge each student to think of an effect, write it on a strip of paper, and place it inside the bag. Then continue in the same manner as before, with students suggesting the causes for these effects.

- Use your current read-aloud to help your students understand more about cause and effect. Have each student choose an event from the story and decide whether it is a cause or an effect. Then instruct the student to determine the corresponding cause or effect for that event. For example, if a student selects a thunderstorm as a cause, he could use "character gets wet" or "flash flood" as possible effects.

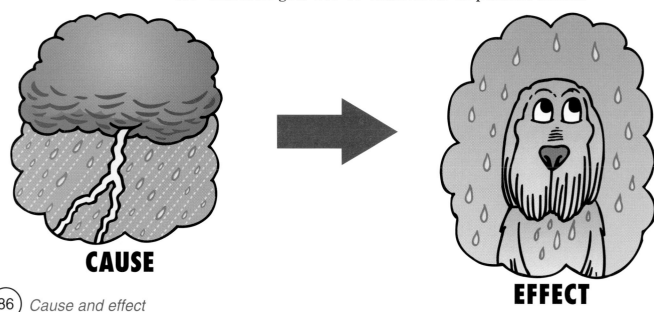

CAUSE

EFFECT

Lights! Camera! Action!

Set the stage for giving and following specific directions with this lesson.

Skill: Writing and following directions accurately

Estimated Lesson Time: 45 minutes

Teacher Preparation:

1. Duplicate a copy of page 89 for each student.
2. Enlarge the figure on the answer key for page 89 on a transparency.
3. Cut sheets of 8 1/2" x 11" scrap paper into four equal squares, enough for each student to have three squares.

Materials:

1 copy of page 89 for each student
a transparency of the enlarged answer-key figure
3 squares of scrap paper for each student

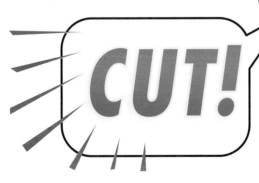

CUT!

Background Information:

Whether cooking or playing a game, giving—and following—directions is important. Directions should always be complete and arranged in a logical order. Certain words can indicate when directions are being given. Such clue words include imperative verbs such as *draw, read, circle, glue, cut, tie, underline,* and *mix.* In addition, sequence words—such as *first, next, then,* and *last*—reveal the order in which the directions should be followed. Numbers can also indicate the sequence of steps.

Sequence Words:

first

next

then

last

Introducing The Lesson:

Begin this lesson by discussing the importance of following directions accurately. Ask students what would happen if a person ignored the directions when she prepared a cake. Challenge your students to give additional examples of situations in which following directions is important. Record your students' responses on the board.

Steps:

1. Explain that in order for someone to follow a set of directions accurately, all steps must be included and written in an understandable way. Point out that directions must be precisely written and in a sequential order for them to be clearly understood. Review specific words that help make directions accurate (see page 87).

2. Give each student a copy of page 89 and instruct him to follow the directions for Part One carefully. Afterward have your students compare their drawings to the one on your transparency.

3. Next go over the directions for Part Two. Challenge your students to write their directions as accurately as possible. Afterward collect your students' completed worksheets.

4. Give each child three squares of paper. Select one of your students' sheets from the papers that you collected. Without showing the drawing on the sheet to the class, explain that you will read aloud the directions for a drawing exactly as they were written by the author.

5. Direct your students to follow these directions as accurately as possible to draw the figure being described. Have them draw the picture on one of their paper squares.

6. Afterward display the original drawing so that your students can make comparisons.

7. If their drawings are very different, discuss whether this is due to errors in writing the directions or in following the oral directions.

8. Repeat this procedure with two more drawings. Conclude the lesson by reviewing the importance of accuracy when giving *and* following directions.

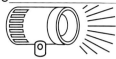

Lights! Camera! Action!

Part One: Follow the directions below to draw a figure on the projection screen at the right.

NOW PLAYING!

Mystery Animal

First, draw a medium-sized circle in the middle of the projection screen. Second, draw two smaller circles outside this circle—one that touches this circle's northeast perimeter and another that touches its northwest perimeter. Next, draw a smaller circle inside each of the circles just drawn. Then draw a small, horizontal oval in the middle of the medium-sized circle. Now draw two small circles side by side and centered just above the oval. Make a dot in the center of each of these small circles. Finally, draw a half circle that is centered below the oval.

Part Two: Draw your own figure on the projection screen to the left. This time write the directions that tell how to draw it as numbered steps.

COMING SOON!

_____

_____

_____

_____

_____

_____

_____

_____

_____

Bonus Box: Write directions that tell how to make your favorite snack on the back of this sheet.

©1997 The Education Center, Inc. • *Lifesaver Lessons*™ • Grade 4 • TEC495 • Key p. 96

How To Extend The Lesson:

- Pair your students; then have each pair create a board game that reviews a concept learned in class. Give each pair a sheet of heavy-duty poster board for designing its game. Then direct the pair to write clear, detailed instructions that explain how to play this game. Afterward allow the pairs to exchange these games and play them.

- Give each student a sheet of unlined paper for writing step-by-step directions that tell how to do her favorite recreational activity. Then direct her to cut her paper so that each step of the activity is on a separate strip. Afterward have the student shuffle her strips and exchange them with a classmate's. Challenge each student to arrange the activity's directions in the correct order. Then direct the original author to check for accuracy.

- Duplicate several simple recipes that would appeal to your students, omitting several important steps. Share these revised recipes with your students, directing them to read the recipes and point out where steps are missing. Together, discuss problems that might arise if the directions are followed as written. Then challenge your students to supply the missing directions.

- Cut a red construction-paper nose for each student. Have each student put a rolled piece of adhesive tape on the back of her paper nose. Then draw a large clown face on your chalkboard. Call one student at a time to come to the board. Blindfold this student; then gently spin her. Have another student give directions to this blindfolded student about where to place the nose on the clown. Afterward allow these two students to judge how well they followed or gave directions based upon the nose's placement on the clown.

A Look Into The Future

Peer into a story's text and illustrations for glimpses of its upcoming events.

Skills: Predicting future events; gathering details from text or illustrations to make predictions

Estimated Lesson Time: 45 minutes

Teacher Preparation:
Duplicate one copy of page 93 for each student.

Materials:
1 copy of page 93 for each student

Background Information:
A *prediction* is a logical guess about a future event or action. In order to make a prediction about what will happen next in a story, the reader must know what has already happened and what is currently taking place in the story.

Making predictions 91

Introducing The Lesson:

Ask your students to predict what would happen in the following situation. Have them imagine that they are scheduled to go outside for a kick-ball game in 15 minutes. But then add that the sky is turning black and loud rumbles of thunder can now be heard in the distance. Allow your students to make several predictions about what will be done about the kick-ball game. Then point out how important it is to thoroughly analyze a situation in order to make a sensible prediction about the future.

Steps:

1. Read a chapter from your current read-aloud, stopping as needed to allow your students to predict upcoming events. Have every student who shares a prediction to explain the details from the story that led him to make that prediction.

2. Ask each student to recall a situation in which she successfully predicted how it would end. Allow several students to share their personal experiences.

3. Explain that predicting the outcome of a story helps a person to understand more about what he reads and thus enjoy it more. Point out that many people make predictions about a story based on personal experiences or their knowledge of the characters and events. Establish that these persons then read on to find out if their predictions are correct.

4. Give each student a copy of page 93.

5. Instruct your students to follow the directions on the reproducible.

A Look Into The Future

Directions: Read each selection below carefully. Then write your prediction about what will happen next on the lines at the base of each crystal ball.

1. Jennifer has an important science test on the same day as the regional soccer finals. She practices soccer every evening until it is time to go to bed. She doesn't study her science notes. When Jennifer takes her science test, she...

PREDICTION:

2. Liz is getting ready to go walking with her friends, but she hasn't done any of her chores. As Liz goes to the door to meet her friends, her mother says...

PREDICTION:

3. Dave and Michelle want to visit a theme park next month, but they have no money. As they walk home from school, they see signs in a neighborhood store window about baby-sitting and cutting grass. Dave and Michelle...

PREDICTION:

4. Ray and Andrew know the rule that all scouts should stay with the group when hiking. But while walking through the canyon, the boys decide to take a shortcut to beat the rest of the pack back to camp. As the sun begins to set, they see no sign of their camp. The boys...

PREDICTION:

5. Sharon arrived on time for her 1:00 hair appointment. Carolyn—the hairdresser—rolled Sharon's hair and applied the perming solution. Then Carolyn got an unexpected phone call and did not return to check on Sharon as scheduled. When Carolyn returned, Sharon's hair...

PREDICTION:

Bonus Box: On the back of this sheet, write an unfinished story similar to those above. Then have a classmate read your story and predict how it will end.

©1997 The Education Center, Inc. • *Lifesaver Lessons*™ • Grade 4 • TEC495 • Key p. 96

How To Extend The Lesson:

• Have each student bring in a favorite novel. Direct each student in turn to share just her book's cover illustration and title with the rest of the class. Then challenge the class to make predictions about each story based only on the information that was given. Then instruct the student to read aloud the book-jacket summary from her book. Afterward have your students compare their predictions with the actual contents of each book.

• Select a short story that is unfamiliar to your students. Begin reading it aloud. Before the story's conflict is resolved, stop reading. Instruct each student to write his own ending to the story. Then have several students read their endings aloud. Afterward read the actual ending of the story to the class.

• Cut out several news stories and their accompanying photos from your local newspaper. Display these photos one at a time; then have your students suggest a photo caption for each photo and predict what could happen next on the pattern below. Remind your students that their predictions must be logical and based on information suggested by the photo. After the predictions for each photo have been made, read its accompanying article aloud. Then have your students discuss how accurate their predictions were.

©1997 The Education Center, Inc. • *Lifesaver Lessons*™ • Grade 4 • TEC495

Answer Keys

Page 4

The first Labor Day parade was held on September 5, 1882, in New York City. Since so many people participated in the events on that day, officials decided to honor workers every year. On June 28, 1894, President Grover Cleveland officially proclaimed the first Monday in September as Labor Day.

Page 5

1. A South American cowboy wears a felt gaucho hat as part of his traditional costume.
   A is the first word in the sentence. *South American* names a specific nationality.

5. In the 1400s, many women in Europe wore a three- to four-foot-tall, veiled, conelike hat known as a *hennin*.
   In is the first word in the sentence. *Europe* names a specific continent.

6. The height of an Amish person's hat—and the width of its brim—revealed whether its wearer was married or not.
   The is the first word in the sentence. *Amish* names a specific group of people.

7. Wearing her graduation cap and gown proudly, Mrs. Jones finally graduated from college at the age of 45.
   Wearing is the first word in the sentence. *Mrs.* is a title. *Jones* names a particular person.

8. People in Scotland wear a hat called a *tam-o'-shanter* as part of their traditional dress.
   People is the first word in the sentence. *Scotland* names a specific country.

9. The first hat factory in the United States was established in 1780 in Danbury, Connecticut, by Zadoc Benedict.
   The is the first word in the sentence. *United States* names a specific country. *Danbury* names a specific city or town. *Connecticut* names a specific state. *Zadoc Benedict* names a specific person.

10. I heard John say that he plans to wear a green hat on St. Patrick's Day in March.
    I is a pronoun that should always be capitalized when it stands alone. *John* names a particular person. *St. Patrick's Day* names a holiday. *March* names a month of the year.

The following hats should be colored because no other words in their sentences need capital letters: 2, 3, 4

Bonus Box: Students' answers will vary, but possible responses could include a beret, sombrero, pelo, gaucho, baseball hat, bonnet, cowboy hat, cap, magician's hat, top hat, crown, and various types of helmets.

Page 9

1. Exclamatory and imperative; Quiet on the set!
2. Interrogative; Is Jennifer Carol the star of this film?
3. Imperative; Please lower the lighting in the room.
4. Interrogative; When does this movie begin showing in theaters?
5. Declarative; Jake Hardy is the director of the movie.
6. Interrogative; How long will it be until the film is completed?
7. Imperative; Take the film to the production room.
8. Declarative; Each scene's number is written on the clapboard.
9. Exclamatory and imperative; Be careful with that expensive scenery!
10. Imperative; Do not talk while the camera is rolling.
11. Exclamatory; This film will bring in millions at the box office!
12. Exclamatory; That's a wrap, folks!

Page 13

1. The pet ate the food.
2. I got a toy on the holiday.
3. The boy used soap to wash the car.
4. The city is in a state.
5. The president went to the store.

Students' sentences with proper nouns will vary.

Page 17

The 15 action verbs are:

gallop	flew	leap
run	see	sleep
eat	explode	understand
think	jump	save
carried	wonder	grew

Students' sentences with these words will vary.

Page 21

SUBJECTS

My little sister and I
Scrappy, the family dog,
The streetlight
Carrie
I
The alarm clock
Aunt Sharon
my bedtime

PREDICATES

go to bed at 9:00 P.M.
keeps me warm.
tell us bedtime stories each night.
is down the hall from ours.

Page 29

1. Goodall's
2. '60
3. chimpanzees'
4. can't
5. swingin'
6. ape's
7. gorilla's
8. aren't
9. Asia's, gibbons'
10. gorillas'

Page 65

A. 1, 3, 2
B. 2, 3, 1
C. 1, 3, 2
D. 1, 3, 2
E. 3, 2, 1
F. 2, 1, 3

Special message: *The order of events is important.*

Page 73

1.
musical instruments
1 cithara
3 mridanga
2 lute

2.
rocks
2 gneiss
3 schist
1 basalt

3.
clothing
3 toga
1 frock
2 jerkin

4.
cloth
3 worsted
1 gabardine
2 voile

5.
sports
2 jai alai
3 quoits
1 falconry

6.
hats
2 petasus
1 beret
3 tricorne

7.
dances
3 lindy
1 bolero
2 cotillion

8.
trees
2 quince
3 upas
1 mimosa

9.
hairstyles
3 marcel
2 cornrow
1 chignon

Bonus Box:
Students' answers will vary.

Page 77

Students' answers will vary, but possible definitions and words to underline are given below.

1. *Newsprint*—coarse paper made from wood pulp on which newspapers are printed.
   Newspapers are printed on/coarse paper made from wood pulp.

2. *Tabloid*—a smaller-sized newspaper that has lots of pictures, larger headlines, and shorter articles than a standard paper.
   half the size of a standard newspaper's pages/lots of pictures, larger headlines, and shorter articles.

3. *Beat Reporters*—reporters who cover news in one particular location or about one particular subject.
   Reporters who cover news in one particular location or about one particular subject are called beat reporters.

4. *Lead*—the first paragraph of a news story.
   the first paragraph, which contains important facts.

5. *Copy Editor*—person who checks a reporter's article for accuracy, writes a headline for it, changes some words to make it easier to understand, or cuts some of it if it is too long.
   someone who checks it for accuracy and writes a headline for it. This person may change some words to make the article easier to understand or cut some information if the story is too long. The person responsible for this job is called a copy editor.

6. *Layout*—a sketch.
   a layout—or sketch—of each newspaper page/where each story, picture, and advertisement will be placed on a page

Bonus Box:
1. after
2. in another sentence
3. before
4. after
5. before; or before and also in another sentence
6. after; or after and also in another sentence

Page 81
1. Opinion
2. Fact   I
3. Fact   S
4. Opinion
5. Opinion
6. Fact   A
7. Opinion
8. Fact   L
9. Opinion
10. Fact   U
11. Fact   A
12. Fact   R
13. Fact   T
14. Opinion
15. Opinion
16. Fact   A

Koalas live in **AUSTRALIA.**

Page 89
Part One:

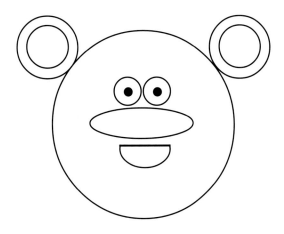

Part Two: Students' directions will vary depending on the figures that are drawn.

Page 93
Students' predictions will vary, but possible responses are:
1. Jennifer does not do well on her science test.
2. Liz's mother tells her she cannot go walking until she finishes her chores.
3. To earn money for the theme park, Michelle gets a job baby-sitting and Dave gets a job cutting grass.
4. Ray and Andrew realize that they are lost.
5. Sharon's hair was too curly. *Or* Sharon's hair was damaged because the perming solution was left on too long.